Ira Sandperl

A
Little
Kinder

Palo Alto, California

Jacket by Saul Shepherd

Library of Congress Card Number 73-93870

ISBN 0-8314-0035-8

Dedication

The original dedication was to be to four men and one woman: Roy Kepler, Peter Szego, Art Hoppe, Francis Heisler and my mother, Ione Sandperl. Their lives of unflagging goodwill ceaselessly sustain me.

But two young women made the book possible. Margaret Moses charged it with love and Tamara Cohn Eskenazi kept it alive and made it grow.

Preface

This book consists of a unique collection of letters written by Ira Sandperl to a young girl of considerable intelligence and perception. The series of letters serves at once to educate the girl "in spite of the formal education she is receiving," and to delineate the early days of the non-violent, civil rights and peace movements when Ira Sandperl was helping Martin Luther King, Joan Baez and eventually hundreds of thousands of people who helped bring American participation in the Vietnam War to an end.

I had the personal good fortune to participate first-hand in one of the experiences described in this book—hearing Ira conduct seminars on Gandhi and Huxley for the rest of us jailbirds in the Santa Rita Jail after the Oakland draft demonstration in 1968.

An unexpected delight for the reader will be Ira's annotated reading list.

Finally, is the girl to whom Ira has written so eloquently real or is she a literary device? Perhaps only Ira Sandperl knows. In any event, she becomes quite real in the pages that follow. Together with her, the reader stands to gain a profound yet easy-to-absorb education.

Robert S. Spitzer, M.D.

Introduction

I met Ira when I was sixteen. My father was still taking us to Quaker meetings. We all hated it, but it never occurred to me not to go, because it was too much of a struggle contending with my father's hurt feelings and the ensuing family disasters. Anyway, there I was, sixteen, squirming through the Sunday morning silences and occasionally teaching the kindergarten class. They call it "first-day school."

One sunny but boring Sunday, as I recall now, there was a funny bearded man at the meetinghouse, and he had a laugh like a goat. He smiled and laughed lots, and his eyes were always filling with tears. He was some kind of legendary person, because most of the kids already knew him. I heard he was going to take over our high school first-day classes. That's all I can remember about the first time I met Ira—that it was sunny, and that he had a laugh like a goat.

He did take our class, and we began to call his sessions the "sermons on the pavement." He talked a lot about Gandhi, and something called nonviolence, and we read from a book by a Chinese philosopher named Lao-tse. One of the things Lao-tse said was, "The is is the was of what shall be," and I thought that that was the cleverest thing I'd ever heard.

I began to grow very fond of the bearded guru with the goat laugh. I felt he might have answers that no one else had. I asked him how I could learn to get along with my sister Mimi. She was twelve then, and very beautiful, and we fought all the time. Not in a big way, but by nasty little put-downs and ugly faces, and once in a while nail marks left in each other's arms. It seemed so endless and unkind. Ira said to pretend that it was the last hour of her life, as, he pointed out, it might well be. So I tried out his plan. Mimi reacted strangely at first, the way anyone does when a blueprint is switched on him without his being consulted. I learned to look at her, and as a result, to see her for the first time. I began to love her. The whole process took about one summer. It's curious, but there is perhaps no one in the world as dear to me as Mimi.

Ira dressed in corduroys and sweatshirts and a baggy duffle coat and a beat-up alpine hat. He began to come by my house on his bicycle every morning before school. I'd skip first period and he'd be late to work, and we'd walk in the morning sun and make jokes about the world, and at the same time I knew that he and I felt desperately that we must do something to try and help the world. My father once asked Ira what he saw in this sixteen-year-old, to visit me every morning. Ira just told him that I was extraordinary.

I began accompanying Ira to places when he spoke. I heard more things about Gandhi and love and nonviolence and a brotherhood of man, which he said didn't exist yet. Once we went to a Jewish junior high school summer camp. Ira spoke, and I sang, and he made some remark to the effect that we would have to travel around doing that someday, and maybe we could make a change in the world.

One day I asked Ira to visit my school, Palo Alto High School. He came to an English class with me, and the teacher was late, so Ira got up and began to answer questions. When the teacher arrived we were talking about life and war and love and nonviolence, and the teacher had the good sense to let us continue. But the administration had heard by now that English 12 had let an agitator loose in front of the kiddies, and Ira and I were called to the front office at the end of the period. The vice-principal waited until the bell had rung for the next class, and then he began to explain to Ira how it was illegal for him to be on the campus without a certain pink pass signed by the principal. I asked him if he could please give us one and he said no he could not, that it had to be applied for by one of the students, and then decided upon by the administration, and would I please go to my class now. I asked him why I should go to my class, and he said because the bell had rung. I said I was staying until my guest left, and the vice-principal said no, no, go back to class, how could I learn anything if I didn't go to class. I told him I was learning something right that minute. I was learning how he and Ira acted with each other. He gave up and just tried to hurry Ira out the door. I took Ira's arm and walked him out of the office and down the hall to the front entrance. I knew the vice-principal was peeking from somewhere so I walked out of the building onto the porch, just to give him a scare, and I shook Ira's hand good-bye. I don't know why I didn't keep walking. It would have been right. The only real teacher at school that day was being kicked off the campus.

Once we went to Dinah's Shack together for dinner. I went barefoot, and he in his regular funny outfit. Dinah's Shack has a smorgasbord, with lots of salads and cheeses, which Ira liked, because he didn't eat meat. I ordered a piece of roast beef and then couldn't eat it. I just ate things off the smorgasbord table. We walked home after dinner, right down about three miles of main highway, and then across the Stanford hayfields, talking and laughing—an intellectual hobo and a gloriously deteriorating remnant of the American public school system. In the middle of the fields I noticed that it seemed that the clouds were moving with us. Ira says that I stopped and said, with great relief, that I was glad my father wasn't there, because he would have had to explain it.

When I went East, at the end of my senior year, I wrote Ira only now and then. He was by then, and remains still such a constant thing to me that it doesn't matter if he is nearby, or in some other state. I knew he was a part of my fate, and it didn't alarm me to sense that.

Ira was born into an affluent family in St. Louis, Missouri. His father was a surgeon. The Sandperls had a home in St. Louis and an apartment in the Plaza Hotel in New York. The images I have from what he's told me of his childhood suggest something equivalent to the story-book heroine, Eloise. There was a maid and a butler who doubled as chauffeur. Ira says he was able to escape from that mold because of his mother. "We were a good Jewish family," he says. "We were allowed to do just about anything but be stupid. We could not be stupid. My mother thought violence was the stupidest thing of all, so I was really a pacifist from a very early age." As a very young man, he was sensitive and wise, gentle, clever, bright, and extremely stubborn. He had the face of a young Indian prince, and an ego to match—all with the added attraction of his limp which came from a case of polio he contracted shortly after he was born. When he went away to Stanford, he sent his shirts home to St. Louis to be laundered, because he couldn't find a laundry on campus that came up to snuff. He dressed in Brooks Brothers clothes, and had affairs with very attractive, usually married women.

Then one day he walked past a bookstore and saw, in the window, a picture of a skinny brown man in a loincloth, sitting at a spinning wheel. Ira had no money with him at the time, but said he would come back and pay for the book the next day if the clerk would let him take it home. The clerk said that anyone interested in that book was not likely to be dishonest, and he gave Ira the book.

"Gandhi, the rat!" says Ira. "He ruined my life!"

Ira fell in love with nonviolence and dropped out of Stanford in order to pursue his education.

Ira is a rascal who longs to be a saint. He is lured by the life of the recluse, by monks' robes and silent hillsides and the nonexistent waters of purification. He longs to be free of earthly ties and desires. He meditates all the time, and carries on what he calls his monologue with God, and then loses his temper in public and chatises himself for hours afterward, putting his hat over his face and groaning to me, "Oh God, I was awful. Just awful. I'll never make it."

So we travel together, teach together, march together, laugh and cry together, sit-in together, and go to jail together. He is an endless joy to me.

Contrary to all outward appearances, Ira and I have never been in love with each other in the conventional sense, and have never had an affair. It has been a spiritual marriage which has brought only the most constructive and tender companionship. One night, during the year of Ira's second marriage, as we sat in the lamp-lit restaurant of some fine hotel in some foreign land, Ira with his Bloody Mary and I with my tomato juice, we had a little exchange of true confessions on why neither of us had ever had the desire to go to bed with the other. I guess we'd never brought it up before because we each felt we would injure the other's ego. We decided that to have had an affair would have been much too dangerous. Neither of us can stand to be on the losing end of anything, and we are both, by nature, hopelessly inconsistent, or more bluntly, fickle. We decided that a safety valve in each of us decided that that was the one person to beware of, and the danger of an imminent fall of pride warded off any sexual attraction. How grateful we both are, because we seem very bad at mixing sex with love over any period of time, and, the nonviolent movement being what it is

x

today—namely, practically nonexistent—would have suffered greatly from the disintegration of one of its most active teams. But nonviolence is stuck with us, and we are stuck with nonviolence. And it's a glorious life, Ira, and I feel terribly lucky to know you.

Joan Baez

Late March
Early April
1971

Please don't be put off because I have not begun this letter with a salutation. It is not because you are not dear to me; I think you know how you stand in my affections. As a matter of fact, I probably will not use salutations in any of this series of letters to you, my extraordinary eighteen-year-old. Why? Because I feel these letters are bound to be more than letters alone.

So. My answer is excitedly, emphatically yes. To be asked to take your education in hand, to be your mentor, to supplement, supplant or subvert what goes on or does not go on at your college delights me beyond measure.

There is always so much to say, and I am always aware that many have said everything better. I am always eager to be simple, always aware how difficult that is and I am not a little annoyed by the ease with which one slips into the pretentious, especially one who has made the bumptious claim of being a teacher.

Yet you have taught me more than I have ever learned before about what it means to be human. So in your new correspondence course I shall no doubt be as much the learner as the educator. For there is no education without complete and lively mutual participation, which does not rule out attentive silence—often the most complete and liveliest participation.

In both these areas the old rascal-sage Socrates failed. He was never silent with his young friends and he did all the participating, continually using his pupils as straw men. I don't intend to do that.

So I want to say that today to you, to me, to the world, I formally renounce the claim of teacher. In the pedagogue's place stands a wayfarer, a traveler, an explorer; a little too timid, but not an out-and-out coward. Sometimes this wayfarer stands stiffly withdrawn. More often he is loosely languid, inclined toward good-humored irony. But sometimes he is all these things alternately or simultaneously.

The pedagogue makes his exit gracefully. It is the perfect morning to make a graceful exit. It is beautiful outside; cloudless, with only the faintest touch of the iodine-colored smog

3

that has become the world's most hideous emblem of the military-industrial uniform— which reminds me that yesterday I saw a handsome young officer in a military uniform I did not recognize. When I asked him, he told me in English that it was German.

"East or West?" I asked.

"West," he said and laughed. The laughter is a good sign. Laughter will make nationalism and uniforms only for musical comedies. The anti-war movement also is far too grim. Officious and self-righteous it, alas, is like its adversary. We need more of the light comedy of Gilbert and Sullivan and less of the coarse bellicosity of science fiction. More of Lao Tze and less of Mao.

I am writing in bed where, in fact, I do most of my writing. Like Proust, but without his asthma, genius or intelligence. I think of him a lot. I think of his love of his mother and his grandmother and it touches me sadly, happily.

At the age of twenty he wrote of his grandmother, "As a result of a miracle of tenderness which had imprisoned my thought in each one of her ideas, of her intentions, of her words, of her smiles and glances, there seemed to exist between us a peculiar, a pre-established harmony, which made of me—her grandson—so much her own possession, and of her—my grandmother—so much mine; that it had been suggested that either of us should have been replaced, she by some woman of superlative genius, I by some man of the noblest sanctity ever known since the world began, we should have smiled, knowing full well that each would have preferred the worst fault of the other to all the virtues to be found in the best of humanity."

Freud must have had a great deal to say about all this. But I'm not sure that Proust's psychology doesn't hold up better than Freud's.

P.S. I do not mean to be running down the venerable Viennese, which seems something of a vogue today. Stay off bandwagons and watch out for unhinged pendulums.

4

To say that the world is endlessly odd is banal, but apt. The satirist has no more a place in our society because he cannot satirize that which is already grotesque. Satire has to be seen as a fine and subtle distortion of a known and accepted measurer of sanity. Such a measure does not exist, least not that we mortals can see.

Perhaps it existed at one time in the mind of Albert Einstein. But then he announced with bitter humor, that had he to live again, he would choose to be a plumber. He made that remark when all of contemporary physics, most of which was his invention, was turning to ashes in his mouth; a poetic and illuminatingly wondrous vision was being fashioned into an arsenal of vulgar and glittering gadgetry of incalculable destruction.

Who in his right mind can doubt the living hand of Satan? Only a more than human diabolical intelligence could have selected Einstein to be the instrument of such cosmic treachery. Einstein of all people! It was a joke of matchless ferocity.

Here was a man of great culture. He loved Bach and Spinoza, had the transparent eyes of a saint, was an authentic pacifist most of his life, and said that "Killing in wartime was no better than common murder . . . Heroism by order, senseless violence, and all the pestilent nonsense that goes by the name of patriotism—how I hate them! War seems to me a mean, contemptible thing. I would rather be hacked to pieces than take part in such abominable business."

And this was the man who made Pandora's box seem like one of the more harmless toys in the nursery! After this, not to believe in the Devil? Not to give him his due? Really! Wars in the name of the Prince of Peace? And this latest refinement taking the inspiration of the gentle genius of our time and making it into the means of apparently limitless slaughter, is an incontestable masterpiece of malevolance.

And yet if Einstein had listened to Pascal, we would today be facing a different, happier world; a different, happier world would be facing us. (Put on your reading list Pascal's *Pensees* and his *Provincial Letters*.)

Over three hundred years ago he explained it to us:

"We make an idol of truth, for truth without charity is not God, but His image and idol, which you must neither love nor worship."

"Charity" was then a word of great nobility, but has now fallen on evil days. It means love, and has nothing to do with individual or organized donations of any kind.

It is clear, appallingly clear, that truth without love has made the pursuit of learning and the centers of learning in the world, a deodorized charnel house. And love without truth has turned the churches, temples, synagogues and mosques, as well as almost all other institutions, into suffocating cloisters, overcrowded moral slums.

To underline what Pascal said, because it is of the greatest importance, I would put in language not made dim by theological idiom.

It is simply that truth without love ceases to be truth and is a seductive, self-righteous, suicidal mirage by which we are deceived until it is too late; and that love without truth is impotent sentimental twaddle. Truth and love, indivisible, scrupulously approximated and concretely applied, are the health and holiness of life. Their absence is the plague of meaninglessness and all its attendant horror and hollowness.

But you ask (and of course rightly, "Miss Pilate") what is truth? What is love? We will not, like Pilate, cynically wash our hands of any part of the question, but join our hands in its exploration.

I am in a rare mood of optimism. We shall understand the understandable, which means we'll understand that we do not understand, and in that, truth and love will show themselves as they are in themselves; not static but always in movement. "It is the journey, not the arrival that matters." And "once and for all" is the illusion and the lure of death and dogma.

Happy "April Fool's" day.

Perhaps this would be the appropriate day for all of us ordinary people of the world to tell the captains of industry, the generals of armies, and the heads of states that we have quietly resigned; that we will not return to work until there are no more frontiers, no more competition, no more exploitation, no more racism, no more poverty, no more male or female chauvinism, no more sexual ostracism, and no more killing. (I have left out gay and women's liberation, not because I think them unimportant, but because they are an integral part of our *human* liberation, that liberation from the entire Bastille of our fears.)—an April Fool's day, in short, to end all foolishness.

An astute man (whenever he was not self-righteously angry) once urged, hoped and thought that the workers of the world would unite, lose their wretched chains, and gain and share the fruits of the earth. It was not so long ago. Only a hundred and twenty-three years have passed since The Communist Manifesto first made its German appearance. The Germans have bestowed an abundant and queer assortment of gifts: Bach, Goethe, Kant, Einstein, Marx, Schopenhauer, Luther, Bismarck and Hitler, to name but the tiniest handful of the most obvious. The roster is weighty, impressive and contradictory.

The Indian philosopher, Radhakrishnan wrote (read his excellent little book, *The Hindu View of Life*): "The human mind in all its baffling strangeness and variety produces contrary types, a Buddha or a Gandhi, a Nero or a Hitler."

It is true. Baffling it is; baffling, maddening, discouraging, heartening, and dramatically exhilarating. My God, we are all made of absolutely the same stuff and we are all not only positively kin, but also we are, *sub specie aeternitatas,* all contemporaries; or more in the spirit of the age: we are all contemporaries in the clear perspective of geological time.

How exciting to be the kin and contemporary of Buddha, Jesus, and Socrates, and at the same time, how salutary and humbling to know that our closest relatives are

7

also Alexander the Great, Ghengis Khan, and Joseph Stalin. I deliberately picked these successful mass murderers who, to this day, are esteemed by great numbers of people in many places of the world. Until such men are viewed with compassion and their deeds with aversion (one of the principal keys of *satyagraha)* we shall tragically go on producing them.

There are Hitlers of the home as well as of the larger world. And there are all degrees of Hitlerdom as there are all degrees of Buddhahood. "It's only a matter of degree," trips off our tongues too often with cavalier dismissal. These degrees are very important because most of us probably will never rid ourselves completely of the Hitler in us, nor cultivate our Buddhahood unflawed.

In short, cruelty and kindness undoubtedly will always be with us. But we can continually diminish the cruelty so it has no lethal or permanently damaging effect, as we continually attempt to be kinder and kinder. Kin and kindness are obviously kindred. When we are aware of this, aware of it in the simple way we are aware of our breathing, which is natural, spontaneous and unself-conscious, "all shall be well." All shall be well, but not perfect. This too we must face; face it gently, lightly, and good-humoredly. There is no perfection, there is only approximation.

"All the exact sciences" Bertrand Russel wrote, "are based upon approximations."

We are a funny, mixed people, living very briefly in a funny, mixed world. It is a joy, often a sorrow, but fundamentally a joy.

That, my girl, is what it's all about, at least to my temporary, approximate understanding at this moment.

Yet, though life is a joy, it is, alas, grim for multitudes of people who are economically impoverished or psychologically enslaved. But it is changing and the struggle is on. And for the first time in history we have all the tools for world-wide well being. And the greatest of these tools is what Gandhi called "satyagraha"—soul force, or truth force. We must learn how to develop and use these tools and become ever more skillfully sensitive craftsmen.

I nsomnia, I'm learning has great advantages such as reading more than usual and taking walks along quiet, deserted streets. No automobiles, or very few, therefore, a small amount of carbon monoxide and little noise, an experience which becomes more precious as it becomes rarer.

Stillness and fresh air have been murdered as mindlessly and indiscriminately as the great herds of bison, and for the same old tiresome, sordid, pathetic reasons: commercial gain and money. And each time we are all poorer for it. My God, how stupid we are! And worse, how afraid. And the fear makes it almost impossible for us to learn from our mistakes, so we either repeat them exactly or dress them in a new, or at least unfamiliar, attire, only to do the same thing all over again. History may not repeat itself, but its facsimiles are superb. It certainly looks as though for the umpteenth time we are fiddling while Rome is burning. But maybe the truth is that Rome has never stopped burning, and we have never stopped fiddling.

Essentially, the horrors have not changed save for names, characters and locations. At least they have not changed since 1914, that hilarious year in which that "war to end all wars" started. And that was the year that laughter went out of the world. Or shall we go back to 1904, to the Japanese-Russian war, when a Japanese officer apologized for accidentally injuring Russian civilians? or to the Franco-Prussian War of 1870 when the Germans would not allow their army to shell Paris? or to . . . no, no, no! Arbitrarily we shall mark the beginning of our present age of technological violence with the so-called First World War. I say "so-called" because it is really a misnomer. In the first place, it was predominantly a western European war whose publicists, with characteristic arrogance (hubris) proclaimed it a world war. Secondly, though there was an armistice and a peace treaty, the war has not come to an end. It may at times have halted a little and become less intense, but it goes on this very day with technically improved fury.

Its major location at the moment is Indo China, but that is by no means its only location. By now the West has made its war into a world war; glorious self-fulfilling prophecy! And when it ends, if it ends, future historians will see it as the Hundred-Years War was seen, as one of a piece, or of myriads and myriads of smashed, inter-related pieces. Of course, there are not the same combatants. The original ones have been maimed, killed, or grown too old as in the Hundred-Years War; but nevertheless, the same unspeakable war continues with the fresh blood of new generations of lovely young people.

When will it end? We do not know. We only know that it began on August 4th, 1914. At the time, the British statesman Sir Edward Grey, watching the lamplighters putting out the gas lights in St. James Park, remarked "The lamps are going out all over Europe; we shall not see them lit again in our lifetime." He was right. He did not. Nor will I. But you, my love, will.

P.S. For your information, there has been, since 1945, an armed conflict on the average of every 5 months, according to George Thayer's *The War Business* (New York, 1969).

Last night I had supper with my old friend, colleague, protege and benefactress, Joan Baez. It was inevitable that she would come to play a part in my letters to you because she has played and plays such a large part in my life. If I had omitted her, it would have been both deliberate and unnatural. And if I had done it, it would have been for two reasons. One, every woman I'm close to is jealous of her. And two, she is already a much over-talked-about public figure. But neither reason has any validity. There is no reason for jealousy on your part. This last sentence would have caused Proust to have winced sadly and incredulously.

Of course he would have been correct. There *is* no reason for jealousy. Unreason is at the very heart of jealousy. No one has matched the infinitely delicate self-torturings of jealousy as in *Remembrance of Things Past*, unless perhaps Tolstoy did, in *Anna Karenina* (an imperative for your reading list), for that old Russian Count Tolstoy knew everything.

Lord, what effrontery or gall or perhaps obtuseness or humility to write for publication after these men have seen it all and said it all! But T. S. Eliot provides the most encouraging rationale. In *The Four Quartets,* in my opinion, the best poem in the English language in the 20th century, he writes:

And what there is to conquer
By strength and submission, has already been
     discovered
Once or twice, or several times, by men whom
     one cannot hope
To emulate—but there is no competition—
There is only the fight to recover what has
     been lost
And found and lost again and again: and now
     under conditions
That seem unpropitious. But perhaps neither
     gain nor loss.
For us, there is only the trying. The
     rest is not our business.

11

Moreover, had other writers been intimidated, book-stores and libraries would have been hugely diminished and the great, never-ending delight in leisurely browsing would have been severely curtailed. And, among stacks and stacks of books, there is always the chance, the undying hope, that one day you will open a book you have never seen before and find that perfect story, chapter, paragraph, sentence or word. Everything will fall into place. And you will exclaim: "Of course! It is obvious! Why did I not think of it all along?" Which was precisely Thomas Huxley's response to Darwin's discoveries. Huxley, after all, was the more learned of the two men. But that is the point, I think. Scholarly expertise, even as broad and deep and original as Thomas Huxley's, often misses the obvious. The genius does not. His experienced eye has somehow retained the newness and wonder of a child's.

> The wonder that I feel is easy
> Yet ease is cause of wonder.

The above is from "Little Gidding" one of T. S. Eliot's *Four Quartets*. The harmony of it, the precision of style, content, humour, wisdom and beauty are an unflaggingly sustained miracle of faultless intensity. And I will boastfully tell you that T. S. Eliot and I have much in common; we were both born in St. Louis, Missouri, and both of our mothers were women. This is surely something the literary critic Edmund Wilson, as well as the conspiracy master J. Edgar Hoover, could have profitably pondered.

At the moment I'm off to have lunch with a young man who has just been released, after 3 years, from a federal prison. His crime was his refusal to be a hired killer, i.e. his refusal to be inducted into the army; his refusal in any way to cooperate with the selective service act, for even to be an official concientious objector to the war would have made him an accomplice to the military servitude of selective service.

Later . . .

Lunch with my young friend was delightful. Prison did not deteriorate him. He in no way liked it, but he gained a depth and a dimension of understanding he had not had before.

And he said he would be willing to go back to prison if necessary, but that this had nothing to do with the romanticism that is involved in any form of violence. I was and am in full agreement with him.

We must take romanticism out of violence, for it is one of its strongest elements. Death, someone else's generally, and the thrill of vicarious or real terror can be made to appear very seductive. Hitler understood this, as did Che Guevara. These killer-lovers—the most deadly of political hybrids—were no fools. And they are both of the right and of the left. And women as well as men. St. Joan and Rosa Luxembourg come quickly to mind.

One of the tasks of the *satyagrahi* is not only to identify this political hybrid, but also make known its harmfulness to itself and to others. But never, never must we underestimate the tragedy and destructiveness of it. Political hybrids, either in masculine or feminine forms, are fatally alluring, especially the more articulate, elegant, handsome, brilliant ones. Their dazzling appeal is that they have first and foremost deceived themselves by renouncing all personal gain and by impressively risking their lives. Then, in the best faith, they have systematically gone on to deceive the rest of us.

We are deceived into believing that we can get the kind of world we seek by doing the very things we are trying to get rid of. "Just a little more violence to end violence." "Just a little more hatred to end hatred." "Just a little more oppression to end oppression"—and on and on.

We are taken in because good people are doing these things, sincere and brave people. And this is why the finer their qualities, the more dangerous they are, the more thoroughly we are fooled.

All the finest qualities in the world cannot change the simple, immutable fact that the ends cannot justify the means, but, on the contrary, the means determine the ends. In all of man's history this stands out clearly and intel-

13

lectually indisputable; yet it has been perversely, insistently, sentimentally and tragically ignored. In this universe the means always and everywhere, without doubt and without exception, cannot, in the very nature of things, but determine the ends. This cannot be repeated often enough (see Aldous Huxley's book *Ends and Means*. Out of print in America, but available in some American bookstores and libraries. It can be ordered from Chatto and Windus in London.)

We get what we do; not what we intend, dream or desire. We simply get what we do. Recognizing this and applying it would, in a generation, bring about the transformation that alone can put an end to the fear, suspicion, and misery which at present hold such terrible sway over all of our lives.

If we see and act upon this (I will say again, unabashedly, what it is—the means determine the ends!), then what the prophets of all ages have wistfully called Utopia will become a reality.

"Nation shall no more lift sword against nation" nor unloose naplam, nerve gas or nuclear weapons. "Neither shall they learn war any more. But they shall sit every man under his vine and under his fig tree; and none shall make them afraid." Because they will have at last understood, because we will all have at last understood, what is required of us." To do justly, and to love mercy, and to walk humbly with "the knowledge that all our means are but temporary ends and that all our ends are but new beginnings. We will have learned what every flower has never forgotten and what all oceans patiently remind us.

With these words of Micah and Sandperl I shall shut up for today. Anyway, no matter what I write, how much or how little, these letters, sometimes windy sometimes breathless, are primarily the messengers of my love.

This is an historically tragic and hallowed day. Three years ago today Martin Luther King Jr. was murdered. And it is Palm Sunday, the day thousands of years ago a brave and doomed young man entered Jerusalem riding a donkey. "Hosanna" (save us now), the crowd shouted in adoration, scattering palms along his path. The donkey, in G. K. Chesterton's poem is made to say:

> Fools! I also had my hour;
>> One far fierce hour and sweet:
> There was a shout about my ears,
>> And palms before my feet.

Jesus rode not a warrior's steed, but the simple creature of the people. Like Gandhi's, Jesus' presence was his dignity. It never depended on what he wore or what he rode.

A bomb was once thrown at an automobile in which Gandhi was riding. He stepped out of the car uninjured. "From now on," he said, "I shall walk everywhere so it will be easier for my assailant to kill me." And many years later, on the day of his assassination in 1948, an American journalist, Margaret Bourke-White (a remarkable woman and a fine photographer; see her autobiography, *Portrait of Myself)* asked Gandhi how he would meet the atom bomb. Would he meet it with nonviolence?

"Ah, ah," he said, "How shall I answer that?" He was working at his spinning wheel as he spoke.

"I would meet it with prayerful action." he said. He emphasized the word 'action;' so the journalist asked what form the action would take.

"I will not go underground," said Gandhi, "I will not go into shelters. I will come out in the open and let the pilot see I have not the face of evil against him. The pilot will not see our faces from his great height, I know. But the longing in our hearts that he will not come to harm would reach up to him and his eyes would be opened. Of those thousands who were done to death in Hiroshima, if they had died with that prayerful action, died openly with that prayer in their hearts, then the war would not have ended as disgracefully as it did. It is a question now whether the victors are really victors or victims . . . because the world is not at peace—it is still more dreadful."

A few hours later, Gandhi met the bullets of his assassin in precisely the manner he said he would meet the atom bomb; openly, prayerfully, fearlessly, hoping that no harm would come to the young man. The assassin had wanted to unite India and Pakistan, not peacefully as Gandhi did, but by a civil war which he thought could take place if Gandhi were dead. There was such a feeling of shock and sorrow in both countries that an Indian-Pakistani war was at least postponed.

In his death as in his life, Gandhi created an atmosphere of peace.

Because I woke up this morning remembering among other things that it was the anniversary of King's assassination, I am going to write you about some of the times he and I were together.

Martin Luther King, one day, years ago in Chicago, asked me to call him Martin. We were walking into the dining room of a dingy motel. At the time we were already good friends. He smiled as he said, "Dr. King makes me feel so stiff and formal and I don't like to feel that way." And in private he usually was neither of these things. He was warm, companionable, young, and sometimes very funny.

I had just handed him a copy of Arnold Toynbee's book *Change and Habit.* I had gotten into the pleasant practice of bringing him a book every time we met. His life was so incredibly full and hectic that I brought him books I thought he may have missed and which would be of particular interest to him. The previous volume I had given him was Dr. Fredrick Wertham's *A Sign For Cain*—an exploration of human violence. Mainly, though not exclusively, it is a study of contemporary violence in America. I'll mention two interesting things that Dr. Wertham points out in the beginning of the book. First, he quotes from the English writer Thomas Hardy: "If a way to the better there be, it exacts a full look at the worst." Secondly, Dr. Wertham makes this personal observation: "I have heard district attorneys asking for the death penalty while pointing to the 'sign of Cain' on the accused's forehead. They did not realize that this sign does not stamp a man as one fit for the death penalty, but on the contrary is a device against continued violence: 'a sign for Cain, lest any finding him should smite him.' "

I had brought Martin the Toynbee volume in part because I liked its whole conception, but principally for the following significant passage: "On the eve of the advent of the atomic age, the Mahatma Gandhi had demonstrated that it's possible to make a revolutionary political change without recourse to the violence that has been customarily used for making politically revolutionary changes in the past. If the human race refrains from committing mass-suicide, it may come, in retrospect, to recognize in Gandhi one of its historic saviors. He may be remembered as the timely prophet of his generation, and the timing of his achievement has surely been providential. In human affairs, change—including revolutionary political change—cannot be arrested or eliminated . . . But the inevitable change need not be brought about by violence, even when the change in question is one of a radical kind that has usually led to bloodshed in the past. There has usually been bloodshed when a subject people has won its freedom from foreign rule and when a subject race has won its emancipation from a dominant race. Yet Gandhi by his revolutionary new political strategy of non-violent non-cooperation made it possible for India and Britain to part from each other in peace and friendship, and Martin Luther King was consciously applying Gandhi's method in his leadership of the ex-African citizens of the United States in their struggle to win equality of human rights with their ex-European fellow citizens. Here is a revolutionary breach with ingrained custom which is making, not for death and evil, but for life and good."

When I gave Martin the book he laughed and said: "Ira, you're trying to make an intellectual out of me."

Laughing in return, I said: "I wouldn't try to do such a terrible thing to anybody."

Joan Baez and I had come to Chicago to discuss with Martin the possibility of jointly beginning seminars on non-violent principles, strategies and tactics in places all over the world, but particularly at that time in the South of the United States. Joan and I had that year established the Institute for the Study of Nonviolence. It was before we moved to Palo Alto in order to have easier access to San Francisco, Berkeley

17

and Oakland. The one advantage of the original location in Carmel Valley, besides the extraordinary beauty, was being surrounded by military installations. So our school gave to a great many young men, for the very first time, the knowledge of the existence of a living, working alternative to the kind of institutions in which they found themselves.

When Joan, Martin and I sat down to lunch, I could not help but notice that at nearby tables, a group of television crews had set up their bulky equipment of lights and cameras. I asked Martin why they were there; our luncheon meeting did not seem that newsworthy.

"I don't know" he said not very happily, "but it happens more and more often, even when I'm not doing anything at all."

"I suppose" I said, "that you or Joan alone, and certainly the two of you together, are always good material for photographing, even if they have to invent a story to go with it. But I'm curious to know their specific assignment. CBS, NBC and ABC just don't casually send their people out to tea, not with all their gear. Do you mind if I ask them what they are doing here?"

"No, I'd like to know." he said.

At the newsmen's tables, I told them why Joan and I were meeting with Dr. King and, as I had fully expected, they were not in the least interested. After a brief, fidgity silence, one man said sheepishly, looking straight at the floor and not at me: "I'll tell you why we're here. We have to be on the spot when someone kills Dr. King. Awful, isn't it?"

"Yes" I said, feeling as if I had been simultaneously struck in the stomach by a fist and a bitter cold wind.

"Ira" Joan said, in that delightful teasing, comic tone I knew so well, when I rejoined them, "have they come to hear you sing?"

"No," I said, managing to respond in kind, "To watch you walk on Lake Michigan."

"They're waiting for me to be killed, aren't they?" Martin said matter-of-factly.

"Yes," I said softly, restraining a deep groan.

"I am not afraid to die," he said

I believe he believed it, but I did not believe it.

Once, when he and I were walking side by side in a

18

march in the South, one of the organizers called out and asked us to walk faster. With disarming light-heartedness Martin's voice sang and echoed through the long line of marchers: "I may be killed, but I am not going to rush."

Later, in our motel room in Chicago, after we had discussed at length our nonviolent seminar plans, Martin concluded in the sonorous voice of the preacher which I have never liked in anyone else but which with him I always found genuine and stirring:

"Ira," he said, "this is an historical meeting and an historical hour. God means us to do great and good things together."

Very moved, I said, "Martin, I don't know anything about that sort of thing. I only hope you are right. There is lots to do." And my hopes were high, for although Martin's God was outside of my understanding, it was not false. He had transfigured that shabby motel room into a place of radiant promise.

And you, my amazing eighteen year old, have often done the same to the chambers of my heart.

Ira

A very private, though not uncommon horror struck yesterday after I wrote you, adding to Palm Sunday and the anniversary of Martin Luther King's assassination. The mother of a young friend of mine committed suicide.

A month or so ago she had come to my apartment. She was in her middle forties, a career woman par excellence. Both she and her daughter thought themselves to be in love with me. More to the unkind point, I recognized that they were both in that upper-middle-class, taut, restless mood that adorns the life of the bored.

She threatened to kill me and I believe she could have done it. I told her either to kill me or to leave, but that I would not go on with our dialogue of low comedy. For, although she was perfectly serious, she was expressing herself with all the triteness of a fatuous and vulgar movie script.

Shakespearian emotion should be accompanied by Shakespearian language, but alas, it seldom is. Our deepest, most genuine emotions are generally uttered in the tongue of some empty-headed trollop. Our authentic howl of anguish comes out a pathetic self-pitying squeak.

I must pause for a moment and reflect on how my words strike you. I can hear your soft voice, "You are heartless, Ira. A woman you knew was desperate enough to take her own life and you are responding with a callousness that you, of all people, deplore."

Not so, my young friend. I ache for her. But her death was as useless and meaningless as her life. She could have changed both, but she chose to do neither. Even the tragedy of her death was on the soap opera level.

Forgive me. I am not heartless. Perhaps it is just that the combination of the anniversary of Martin's death and her own pathetic demise has temporarily replaced my sympathy with a futile anger. It is simply too much; the kinds of things that we do to ourselves and that we let society do to us.

Nevertheless, it was in part this humiliating incongruity between the depth of emotion she was obviously experiencing and her inability to articulate it that made me soften even more toward her. I tried to reassure her within the limits of

20

truth as well as kindness. For I absolutely insist, even in the extreme circumstance that a lie, even the whitest of the genre, does not help anyone. It can never heal or bring anything approaching peace of mind. On the contrary, it is an insult. At its roots is a patronizing or ingenuous (it makes no difference) lack of faith in oneself and in whomever one's addressing. And it is mistrust and fear (inseparable, almost indistinguishable companions) that divide us from ourselves and from others in the most profoundly subtle ways. Nevertheless, compassion is in order for all of us when we speak untruths, for it is compassion and compassion alone (not to be confused with the mawkishness of well-intended lies) that helps us gain the simple demanding courage that it takes to tell the truth.

"A seeker after truth" Gandhi insisted, "has to be as tender as a lotus and as hard as granite." And, of course he meant simultaneously.

Difficult, difficult, difficult, but no one said the journey was going to be easy. And "it is the journey," as I think I have once before quoted form Montaigne, "that matters, not the arrival."

Now to return to the poor woman who committed suicide. As I said, I tried to reassure her, about herself, her daughter, and to some extent about myself. None of the things she and I were discussing touched, I know, the real nature of her anguish. She just became quietly more desperate. Thoreau's phrase "lives of quiet desperation" is the perfect phrase for her and for our era.

What was her real anguish? That too was sad, commonplace. She was an attractive, intelligent woman and by all conventional standards a success. Yet she felt her life meaningless and was miserable. I suggested that there were many interesting things open to her. She smiled, apologized for threatening me and said she was feeling much better. Sorrowfully, I knew she was lying. I never saw her again.

I wish this letter had a happy ending.

21

Death seems to be haunting me of late. Perhaps for that reason I am reading *The Journey Not the Arrival Matters,* the fourth and last volume of Leonard Woolf's autobiography. All four volumes are worth reading, but I would guess that the last one, covering the late '60's would interest you the most. (Harcourt-Brace publishes them all.)

Leonard Woolf was the husband of the celebrated British novelist Virginia Woolf. He died recently, in his early nineties, shortly after the publication of the final volume of his autobiography. His wife Virginia died in 1941 by drowning herself in a river. She feared, not without reason, that she was literally once again going out of her mind. She left Leonard an exquisite, indeed a perfect note, making it clear that their life together had been her greatest happiness. Suicide, nevertheless, if you leave behind people close to you, is a cowardly act carried out by a brave person.

As is almost habitual with me, this is not what I intended to write to you this morning. But, what I laughingly and indulgently call 'my mind,' dances a surprisingly different dance when a pen becomes its maestro. I think this is undoubtedly true for many people and it is an amusing and often pleasant caprice.

I was going to write you of Montaigne, the great 16th century French essayist. Leonard Woolf reminded me of him. Not only did he take the title of the last volume of his autobiography from Montaigne, but he also considered him one of the four most civilized men who ever lived. The other three were Voltaire (*Candide*), Erasmus (*In Praise of Folly*) and Thomas Paine (*The Rights of Man*). On the strength of his autobiography, I would add Leonard Woolf to this distinguished list.

I suggest you read everything Montaine ever wrote; however, I think that the third *Book of Essays* is his best.

Although Montaigne was writing during the time of the inquisition, he wrote prudently but emphatically against it. "After all," he said, "it is rating one's conjectures at a very high price to roast a man alive on the strength of them." Imagine implying that holy writ was conjecture!

Furthermore, he explicitly denounced torture by saying: "I think there is no more barbarity in eating a man alive than in eating him dead. And in tearing by tortures and the rack a body still full of feelings, in roasting a man bit by bit . . . (as we have not only read but seen within fresh memory, not among ancient enemies, but among neighbors and fellow citizens, and what is worse, on the pretext of piety and religion) than in roasting and eating him after he is dead."

To his everlasting credit and courage these were bold and glorious statements for a Frenchman to have published at that time and place, for he surely risked being called in front of the inquisition himself.

Montaigne's deep compassion extended to animals as well. In a beautiful passage he wrote: "Amongst all other vices, there is none I hate more than cruelty . . . if I see a chicken's head pulled off, a pig stuck, I cannot choose but grieve, and I cannot well endure a helpless, dew-bedabbled hare to groan when she is seized upon by hounds."

How rare among Christians! Who else comes to mind besides St. Francis and Albert Schweitzer?

Donald Frame has written a good, but far from lively biography of Montaigne. It is called *Montaigne,* which is perfectly indicative of the book: accurate but unimaginative.

"Had we but world enough and time."

That is the beginning of Andrew Marvel's beautiful and humorous poem, "To His Coy Mistress." With the same feeling I have now, with the same feeling that millions of people must have on awakening, I began another letter with the same poem of Marvel's:

"But at my back I always hear
Time's winged Chariot hurrying near."

Perhaps time is on my mind this morning because I am thinking of you and missing you even more poignantly than usual. Your letter responding to mine about my friend's suicide was graciously fast and shows me once more the fact that you know superbly well one of the few things that count, and which seems, at the moment, in sad decline. You know how to live with extraordinary kindness. That is the real art, the knowledge that passeth all understanding. It's a delicate juggling act of keeping many balls in the air at one time: boldness, strength, forthrightness, awareness, forbearance (something beyond forgiveness), and humility. I have seldom seen you drop any of these. But thank God you have, or you would be more intolerable than you are, with no redeeming faults.

Aldous Huxley is reported to have said: "It's a bit embarrassing to have been concerned with the human problem all one's life and find at the end that one has no more to offer by way of advice that 'Try to be a little kinder.'" You do just that.

Aldous Huxley died of cancer the day John Kennedy was assassinated. And most people know of him because of his novel *Brave New World,* which is on every school reading list, although the novel was not his best medium. He is, however, an essayist of genius, one of the few peers of Montaigne of whom I just wrote you. His was one of the most abundantly and fantastically well-stocked minds of the century—any century. Besides, it was a mind that was disciplined, unpretentious, and delightfully witty.

The Russian composer Igor Stravinsky said that after he and Huxley became good friends, he gave away all his

24

encyclopedias and simply asked Huxley whatever he wanted to know.

All of Huxley's many friends apparently adored him. His conversation was fascinating. He was enormously funny and generous. And most remarkable of all, he took his own advice and always attempted a spontaneous kindness.

In the 9th century, the Chinese poet Po Chui wrote:

> "In the affairs of others, even fools are wise;
> In their own business, even sages err."

But that was not the case with Huxley. He married twice—his first wife died of cancer. And this man had two good marriages whereas most of us can't even have one good one. His second wife, Laura Huxley, wrote in one of her books that Aldous' good will was never absent. Imagine a wife writing that of a husband! Imagine that being true of anyone!

I spent an evening with him many years ago in Palo Alto when he was a guest of the Creative Writing Department at Stanford University.

The evening with Aldous Huxley is among the most pleasant of my recollections. Through his writings he is among the three persons who powerfully fashion my life. The other two, as you know, are my mother and Mahatma Gandhi. I literally cannot imagine what I would have been without them. They are the inexhaustible providers of my physical, moral, spiritual and intellectual well-being, and I am inexpressibly grateful to them.

I have told mother this many times. I never met Gandhi. He was dead one year when he entered and altered my life at the age of 26, as I was innocently reading his autobiography, *My Experiments With Truth.*

But that evening in Palo Alto, I did get to tell Aldous Huxley of my debt to him and thank him for it.

"No," he said, "Thank *you*, for telling me."

It could have gone on like that for hours, but I changed the subject by asking him something I had wanted to know for a long time.

"Why did the discipline and morality of ahimsa, non-killing, nonviolence, which plays a major part in Buddhism, drop from it when it reached Japan in its Zen form?"

Huxley answered as he frequently answered that evening: "I don't know. It was an historical tragedy, but Japan is a strange country."

His genuine unpretentiousness was as impressive as his far-flung intellect. His casual erudition and the unostentatious and remarkable grace of his mind gave a glimpse of what it means to be civilized.

At the barest minimum, read Aldous Huxley's volume of essays, *Tomorrow and Tomorrow and Tomorrow* (New York 1952). The depth, humour, information, and insights are incredible. Read his historical biography *Grey Eminence*: it is 17th century France, the forming of the scourge of political nationalism from which we are still reeling. The grey eminence is Father Joseph, a contemplative who used his powers of meditation for power politics. The right-hand man, no, definitely the left-hand man of Cardinal Richelieu; he did Richelieu's most sinister work, and did it well. Which once again shows we can deploy the noblest disciplines for the lowest practices. This book is so felicitously written, it should be a model for all serious historians and biographers.

And read at least these two novels of his. Huxley is generally not thought of as a good novelist. I do not share this view. He regarded his novels as animated essays. They are that, but a great deal more besides.

Time Must Have a Stop (New York, 1944) is a brilliant, not un-sexy novel dealing with time and eternity. And his last novel, *Island,* (New York, 1962) is a happy, intelligent utopia, making the best of all the worlds and eliminating not only the worst in all the worlds, but eliminating even the mean, petty, everyday numberless stupidities. The heartbreaking element of the book is that we could actually have such a world, provided we were intelligent, civil, unafraid, compassionate, and seriously wanted such a world.

*Mid to
Late April
1971*

W hat a happy surprise to get your letter!

This is neither an implied complaint, nor a masked criticism, just an exuberant exclamation of fact. I know your schedule is full.

I'm delighted that you are pleased with your classes. Especially delighted by the sculpturing. It is one of the great things to do. It is surely one of the best ways of discovering— yourself, the earth with its almost infinite inconceivable relationships, and your relationship to it: body, mind and spirit. Your hands will lay bare the thousand beautiful forms that are waiting there for the artist to make visible, so those of us who do not have that gift can share in it. Universes within universes without end.

The discovery of beauty is always a simple discovery. The discovery of a rock most of us have passed by, a star we were too preoccupied to look at, a glance we pretended not to see, a dandelion someone had said was a weed. Beauty is always that which is first-hand, cannot be copied, reproduced or repeated. It is like falling in love. It is falling in love.)

I loved your letter. I would like to see your sculpture. I'm glad that we have our lives to share, but I miss not being able to reach out my hand and touch you, and you in turn, touch me.

That saying "flattery will get you nowhere," is nonsense. Flattery will get you anywhere. You just better be damned sure you know where you want it to get you.

This is to tell you that the flattery in your letter (which I know you did not intend as such) that my "correspondence course" is better than anything you are learning in college, and that you are sharing it with a number of other students, is most pleasant to hear.

Of course there is excellent precedent for our school of letters. Characteristically I place myself in elegant company. It is not so much a desire to enter, unannounced and uninvited, into a select circle, but to acknowledge my forebears and pay respects to my betters.

I will name some illustrious predecessors who come immediately to mind.

Fenelon, an extraordinary Frenchman (1651-1715) who, besides being the archbishop of Cambrai and a man of parts, was a tireless and exquisite letter-writer. Read Fenelon's *Letters of Love and Counsel* (New York, 1964). It also contains a good essay on Fenelon by my late Trappist monk friend Thomas Merton.

Lord Chesterfield, an 18th century earl, wrote amusing, self-consciously instructive letters to his bastard son Philip Stanhope. There are many editions available.

Rilke's *Letters to a Young Poet,* which has little to do with poetry, but a great deal to do with being young, would be, I think of unusual and pertinent interest to you. Rainer Maria Rilke was an interesting, affected, fragile man born in the 19th century in the beautiful and tragic city of Prague. At the time Prague was part of the Austro-Hungarian Empire, and he was raised in a catholic, German-speaking family. He lived into the twenties of this century, traveled restlessly through Europe and wrote of some of the best poetry in the German language.

Jawaharlal Nehru, the first prime minister of modern India, wrote a large collection of letters to his daughter, Indira, the current prime minister of India. His book was brought out under the title of *Glimpses of World History* (New York, 1942.)

Nehru was often in jail, often separated from his daughter. He wrote the letters from various jails in India, from 1930 to 1933. At the time Nehru was a young man struggling nonviolently with himself and against the British rule of India. His letters have an incredible scope; at once social, political, historical and sometimes touchingly personal. I regretted his becoming a prime minister. A great and forceful and sensitive thinker was lost. And a thinker of that quality is much more important to the good health of the world than the loftiest governmental office-holder. (This happily reminds me of Montaigne's delightfully sobering comment: "Perched on the loftiest throne in the world, we're still sitting on our behind.")

And the last of our predecessors I'm going to mention is Mahatma Gandhi. He wrote a little book called *From Yeravada Mandir.* These are also letters from prison, memorable pieces written in 1930 to his fellow workers at the Satyagraha ashram.

Satyagraha is a combining of two Sanskrit words, satya (truth) and graha (adherence to), Gandhi at various times translated it as "truth force," "soul force" or "that force which is born of truth, love, or nonviolence." The word has a beauty, clarity and dynamic quality that is lacking in the term "nonviolence." It seems logical that Gandhi had to invent an entirely new word for an entirely new concept.

In 1910, the American psychologist, William James, wrote that we would have to discover "The Moral Equivalent to War" if we were to preserve the human race. Satyagraha is that moral equivalent. It is here, and if we can grasp it, understand it, and imaginatively apply it, we can save our world that is now a prisoner of war awaiting its universal death sentence.

These particular letters of Gandhi are the profoundest and most moving writing that this astonishingly marvelous old man ever did. You can get the book from Greenleaf Books, South Acworth, New Hampshire.

How many American flags one sees these days; on the windows of houses and automobiles—and often with the savage, tribal caption: Love it or Leave it. And in China we'd be seeing millions of little red books and blown up photographs of Chairman Mao.

How right the ancient Hebrews were in their powerful warnings against idolatry, how much worse off are we all not to have heeded them. And today the most slavishly adored idol is political nationalism. At present it has 135 allegedly different forms, and as I write this more are coming into being. And although the forms do have some variations, and some are distinctly less hideous than others, it is their almost unchecked military commonality which, unless renounced, will destroy us. (What great idealogue will tell us the difference between a capitalist and a communist nuclear warhead?)

And it is a paradoxical, suicidal ritual that all the wor-shippers are expected, if called upon, to fulfill: defend their idols without question. And all the idols, it turns out, no matter what their shape, design, name or locale, have the same bloody offering of human sacrifices.

So in the end, if there is an end brought about by mutual slaughter, it will not be because the worshippers disagree with one another, but precisely because they are in the most total and primitive agreement. At the right time, in the right uniform, with the right orders, they can merrily murder each other across properly designated frontiers.

But that childish mentality will yet cease to exist, my love. And we'll have roads and meadows instead of frontiers, and we shall meet each other with flowers instead of bombs. The early hippies were this century's most practical realists.

H appy Easter!

Easter, it may come as a surprise to you, was an ancient Germanic goddess of spring. And the Christian feast of Easter corresponds to the older Jewish festival of Passover, which in pre-Mosaic times, must have been simply a celebration of spring. So even in those far-off days Germans, Jews and Christians, were somehow hopelessly scrambled. Racial purity, even if such a thing made sense, which it does not, is an impossibility.

After some time the Passover holiday lost its emphasis on the spring and became identified with the Israelites' exodus from the slavery of Egypt—one of the first historical freedom marches.

"I am the Lord thy God which brought thee out of the land of Egypt, from the house of bondage."

That would have been fine if that was as far as it had gone. But that ferocious old Bronze-age God could not let it go at that. Passover meant sparing the Hebrews all the sadistic surprises he had in store for the Egyptians: from out-and-out germ warfare to the murder of every first-born. And to show that he really meant business, that he literally meant all of the first born, without squeamish, sentimental exceptions "he smote the first born of Pharoh that sat on his throne unto the first born of the captive that was in the dungeon; and all the first born of cattle." If nothing else, God was a thorough-going democrat who must have been a constant inspiration to a man like General Patton. "There was not a house where there was not one dead."

And that, my young friend has come down to us in a book that we are told is holy. Imagine the kindly folk of the West being outraged by Mao's little red book—a kiddies' primer by comparison—a Chinese version of Dick and Jane.

And to complete this charming idyll, let me tell you that during Easter, as well as during Christmas, up through the 20th century until the Nazis put a stop to it, no Jew—young or old—dared to walk the village streets, particularly in Eastern Europe, for fear of being beaten up or killed by his Christian neighbors, celebrating the holidays of the Prince of

33

Peace. As is well known, the Nazis eliminated this barbaric practice by the characteristic Teutonic mercy of eliminating the Jews. It seems no empty boast to claim that we are made in God's image.

And yet, in spite of all the real savagery and trenchant sarcasm, I am in love with the goddess of spring. Her California fragrance is not unlike that of the south of France—a little more tart perhaps.

Yes, I like Easter, I like the idea of resurrection (with a small 'r'), of rising again, out of season as well as in; of beginning anew, of fresh greenery, of dew-wet grass, of smiling boys and girls, of light spring frocks, and not to be left out, of course, the very special, gaily painted Easter eggs whose legend no one knows—a gift of life carried in straw lined baskets.

T his is going to be a personal "newsy" letter, or my attempt at one. I have just realized that I seldom tell you what I feel or what I do; especially I do not tell you what I do. Maybe that is because you really know what I do, and that, by the world's standards, certainly by American standards, I do damn little.

I walk, read, write, reflect and lecture, and of course there is my peace work (which is embarassing when there is no peace). I visit bookstores, art galleries, and listen to a great deal of music. In general, my happiest moments are spent in casual hobnobbing. Perhaps "not doing" things is what I like to do best of all—very unAmerican, I'm sure. I am not a recluse; but I do not like being with many people at one time.

When there is no more war, exploitation, poverty or misery (of a socially planned nature), I am going to spend all of my time in "not doing." And I am going to do my not doing in what Bertrand Russell called "cultured leisure." And I'm going to do it principally, though not exclusively, in Paris, Rome and Venice, with short visits to all parts of the earth.

Occasionally I shall spend a few weeks in the Italian and French countryside. I'm a happy visitor to the country, but really at home in the beautiful old European cities.

It is said that Venice is slipping slowly into its canals. It should, and I am certain can be, stopped. (Read John Ruskin's two volume edition of *Stones of Venice*. The prose of the English language has never been wrought with greater splendor than Ruskin at his best.) It would be an outrageous crime to permit Venice to decay and vanish. But even its sinking is being done in quiet elegance. This is how I would choose to decay: sink and vanish.

So that is the not doing I'm going to do when there is no more war, exploitation, poverty and misery.

In the meantime, I will remain in America attempting to do my infinitesmal part to bring that world into being. (Mr. Gandhi put it well; "No matter how insignificant the thing you have to do may seem, the important thing is to do it.")

And that world is not an impossibility, just unlikely.

And America is the right place to be at the moment. It is the aggressive center of things, and because of that perhaps the most hopeful location to attempt our *satyagraha*.

Once when I was in jail for having committed nonviolent civil disobedience against the war in Vietnam, I thought that if the situation of this country ever seemed absolutely hopeless in terms of nonviolent change I would leave for Western Europe. At the time I was talking with two black fellow-inmates. One was saying he was sick and tired of living in Oakland, California, and that when he got out of jail he was going to leave all this behind. I asked him where he wanted to go.

"Los Angeles, man, Los Angeles," he said.

It was at once funny and sad. And I thought if that seemed to him to be his only alternative, I did not, because I was white, middle-class and privileged, get to go to Europe to live. In short, I did not get to desert him.

Visiting other places from time to time, yes. But no running away; not until everything is all right for every one everywhere. And I thought, too: what if Albert Einstein, Thomas Mann, Bertholt Brecht, and hosts of others had not fled Nazi Germany? What if they had stayed, these men of great international eminence, and had fought nonviolently the mass insanity of Germany? Would that have made a difference? Perhaps. Perhaps not. We will never know. Running away has never solved any social problems, although it has certainly appeared at times to have helped solve personal ones. And to want to run away is humanly understandable. No one gets to condemn anyone for it—we've had enough of condemnations.

Yesterday I did not write you because I thought it was today. Not until late yeaterday afternoon at the post office did I find out the correct date. I thought yesterday was April 15th, the annual deadline for income tax returns. I went madly about getting everything in order not to pay the 63% of the income tax which goes to the military: the cost of past, present and future wars. I wanted to submit my tax form on time so it would be clear that my war tax protest did not get confused with common forgetfullness or willful evasion. I wanted the people in the internal Revenue Service to know that I happily (or at least not too unhappily) pay promptly and fully that portion of my income tax which does not contribute to what R. J. Barnett calls *The Economy of Death* (it is a book which is grisly, full of facts and worth reading.)

Moreover, I'm not an anarchist, opposed to all laws and taxes. I'm opposed to them when they in any way injure, harm, or destroy life rather than sustain and enhance it. The anarchist, however, has a good case, because almost all the laws are designed to preserve the status quo, and the status quo is, without question, the world over helping the rich to become richer and the poor to sink deeper into poverty.

In a world where we TOOK SERIOUSLY the precept that all men are brothers, the tax structure would be one of the first things that would have to be completely overhauled.

As a beginning, for example, we would not need a penny for the now non-existent military (do not forget, this is in a world of applied brotherhood) except perhaps to maintain museums to exhibit the quaint and ingenious artifacts of the bygone age of technological barbarism (hopefully, the young viewers will regard our pre-human ways more with amazed compassion than with scorn). And our taxation would genuinely meet all of our human needs rather than bolster individual national governments and their interlocking consortiums. All of us throughout the world would be helping to support ourselves to live healthy, cooperative, interesting lives, encouraging all of the non-destructive elements of our diverse cultures.

It is the astonishing cultural diversities that are endlessly

37

fascinating; endlessly instructive. We do not have to be the prisoners nor the victims of our or anyone else's culture. We can be the guests and inhabitants of them all.

The Russian poet, Boris Pasternak, said a very beautiful thing: "We are all guests of existence."

If we but realized it, how sensitive it would make us, how unpretentious. We would know that we were only here for a brief time, that we knew very little about ourselves, our fellow guests or our host, the earth. But that, with some patience, some courtesy, some deference, never taking anything for granted, we could learn something from and about each other. How quickly that self-righteous bully in all of us, who knows everything and what is good for everyone, would disappear.

But today the reverse is taking place. We regard ourselves as masters, not guests, of existence, who know what is best for everyone and are using almost all of our resources not for life and diversity but for death and uniformity.

That is why I do not pay the taxes that go for armaments and why you did not get a letter yesterday. I will not give them the money. They have to come and get it. There is a difference, a slight difference, and more and more people understand it, so that one day our treasury will be where our hearts are, and our hearts will be where hearts are meant to be: in love.

The rains washed the smog from the skies. Today appears almost like a beautiful pre-World War II day in California when some people came here for the fine, clear light, and others for quiet, comfortable warmth. One thing I like better today than in former times: fewer people are coming here to die and more are coming to live.

Native Californians (that is, those conglomerate descendants of Europeans who have replaced the Spaniards who have replaced the Mexicans who have replaced the Indians) complain that too many people are coming to California and that, of course, "things aren't what they used to be."

I suppose these complaints are justified, for even I, who have only been here off and on, for thirty years, see too many parking lots and ugly buildings (I live in one) where lovely orchards and meadows used to be.

But we "old-timers," if we were honest, would admit that we like to complain to each other as we smile ruefully and reminisce wistfully. It is one of the curiously pleasant pasttimes as well as one of the sure signs of advancing age.

"What we could divulge, what we could tell of the old place," we chuckle and whisper in a superior fashion. The truth is that what we could say would be of little interest to anyone but ourselves who already know all the queer, really tiresome, commonplace gossip. Thirty years ago when I first came here to go to Stanford University, people were saying exactly the same things that people are still saying: "You should have come thirty years earlier. Then Palo Alto was something special; a fine place to live."

As I was eighteen at the time, I was generously forgiven my poor sense of timing. Naturally, I blamed my parents for it, as I did for every other defect in my character and circumstance. Being a moderately well-read young man, I had read just enough Freud and company to enjoy the profoundly comforting knowledge that my everlastingly inept and irreparable toilet training forced upon me by a furtive and compulsive filicidal father and by an incestuous possessive mother, made it impossible for me to have one shred of personal responsibility. (Read Sophocles and all the rest of that ancient Greek gang. They went through this; in fact, they went through practically everything and recorded it with depth and good taste).

Then did I experience the pleasures of freedom? No; alas, freedom I knew not. One painfully discovers that that clever mountebank, that skillfully disguised imposter is license, the slave master *par excellence*.

Damn! We are all bargain hunters in the never closing chain stores of our desires. And the bargain we really seek is to get something for nothing. But it's an impossibility. Pay we must! And it's not just some conventional or enobling morality. It is simply, naturally, organically, universally the way it is. And whether we like it or not, of course, makes no difference.

And although we are raised to be bargain hunters, raised to want everything for nothing, it is the cost—the capacity to pay—that, I am convinced, brings the most lasting joy.

The cost of our freedom is the deepening, quickening and widening of our fearlessness.

Etymologically, freedom in the English language comes from the two words: peace and love. Without peace and love there is no freedom; it is obvious. Too obvious. R. D. Laing would suggest that is why we overlook it. (His book *Politics of Experience* is worth reading.)

And we Americans who talk so much of freedom (we have turned it into a slogan for fighting wars of domination) should know that the most fundamental freedom is the freedom to live, without which the others can only be a mockery. And yet this pounding insistence on freedom always disturbingly brings to mind Unamuno's gentle but biting remark: "Only the slave talks of freedom, the free man talks of love."

It is very early morning, a little past four, and it is pleasantly dark. The only sounds are birds singing, the faint far-off rumbling of giant trucks on the highway, the muffled humming of distant jet airliners, the deep jolting of freight trains, and the slow slumbering beat of the spring rains. This last produces the cosiest of feelings, provided that one is snugly inside and unaware that the rain is depositing varying quantities of radioactive fallout from thermonuclear bomb tests that the peace-loving countries of the East and West have carried out to insure our safety, prestige, bone cancer and leukemia. (You'll be happy to learn that even these highly sophisticated weapons are becoming increasingly inexpensive to manufacture.)

It is one thing to have lumbered clumsily onto the moon, removing it forever from poetry, but literally to have poisoned the atmosphere for generations to come with the latest science kit from Woolworth's seems to have raised the "boys will be boys" attitude to a magnitude of criminal lunacy.

And yet
And yet
And yet

Basho, the 17th century Japanese poet, wrote these words when his young son died. And I have always found them strangely, powerfully moving. In my mind they are rounded off by William Blake's:

To see a world in a grain of sand
And a heaven in a wild flower,
Hold infinity in the palm of your hand
And eternity in an hour.

So there we are, or where are we?

Despair? Because there is always one more box within the box we thought was the last box? No. The very opposite. Joy. Joy, discovery and patience until the end of our days. Boredom never! For the search always leads us to more search. As the late Gertrude Stein would have said: The

41

search is the search is the search. And for once I would agree with her. At a time of extravagant leisure, you might read her *Autobiography of Alice B. Toklas.* It's particularly pleasant to read aloud.

There is a story of Gertrude Stein's deathroom scene. It is much too good or too clever or characteristic to be anything but apocryphal: It is in Paris in 1946. She is 72. Dying, but holding court as usual, she is surrounded by her illustrious friends, including Pablo Picasso. It is she who breaks the silence.

"Well," she asks, "what is the answer?"

When no one responds, she says: "Well, what is the question?" and dies.

What a question to pose!

You did have the kindness, good sense, discretion, or what you will, to add that I need not necessarily answer because you asked. Well, in theory (and, I know, in all honesty) you have given me an option and an out. The pedagogical propensities of my nautre, or to say it less pompously and more elegantly: my eagerness to follow what Einstein called "holy curiosity," to accept an intellectual challenge, give me, in fact, no choice at all. In Schopenhauer's words: "We can do what we will, but we cannot will what we will." Or, at last, more bluntly, but still procrastinatingly, I'm delighted to try to answer your question "what is love?"

Well, throw open your windows and stand outside on your balcony and shout with all your might into the bracing New England wind, that there is a mad man in California (where else?—but Sinai, Galilee, or the Himalayas) who dares to tell what love is and what it is not. But let me qualify his immodesty and madness by saying that he knows it more by its absence than by its presence.

First of all, there is but one love.

Different kinds of love—agape, philia, eros, profane love and sacred love—all that is philosophical, philogical pious nonsense. For a moment I am back with Gertrude Stein: Love is love is love is love. And, at her side you will find, curious even for that celebrated collector of celebrities, the 17th century prince-bishop of Geneva, St. Francis de Sales (see his *Introduction to the Devout Life*).

"There are many besides you," deSales said, "who want me to tell them of methods and secret ways . . . but the only way of obtaining love is by loving. You learn to speak by speaking, to study by studying, to run by running, to work by working, and just so you learn to love . . . by loving. All those who think to learn in any other way deceive themselves. If you want to love, go on loving more and more. Begin as a mere apprentice and the very power of love will lead you on to become a master in the art. Those who make the most progress will continually press on, never believing themselves to

43

have reached the end."

"Yes, that is all very well," I can hear you saying, "but what is the love you learn by loving?"

It is a gift. A gift of our lives.

For example—and this is neither myth, nor metaphysics, nor poetry—old Gandhi's life could not be taken. He literally gave it away every day, every moment. His life was perpetually up for grabs. He gave it to his assassin. He gave it to everyone he approached. No one could snatch it from him, for he had already placed it in their hands. Whereas most of us fearfully cling to our lives in the illusion that we are loving.

Nevertheless, if we can significantly diminish our fears, we can make a slight gift of ourselves; that unique gift that only we can give. For no matter how long the world spins or the sun shines we will never reappear on the face of the earth So we must be ourselves to give ourselves.

And love is giving ourselves effortlessly, without asking or desiring anything in return. And shared love is a miracle of the communion of uniqueness.

Your capacity for work, your skill in organizing your time is impressive. You get things done that you need to get done, and at the same time you do things you want to do. And the cleverest of all, the two categories are often identical. That's really good. You set me an excellent example. You're turning out to be your mentor's mentor.

Your example could have benefited that unfortunately brilliant and extraordinarily forceful apostle who, in reality, was the inventor or destroyer (perhaps both) of Christianity.

"For the good that I would, I do not! but the evil which I would not, that I do." Poor half-crazed St. Paul. How awful he must have felt when he wrote that (what an excruciating moral hangover!). How awful we all feel when we do precisely that. And it's so damned easy. We clear our own trails, draw up our own charts, and walk straight into our own traps. And not once, but over and over again. Homo sapiens, indeed! What pomposity! If we can not agree on something more modest, we can at least make an appeal for exactness, such as homo inconsistroialis.

But to return to that reformed tentmaker, Saul of Tarsus. He is one of providence's prodigious wreckers, one of its monumental jokes in the worst taste, the kind of joke which compels laughter but at everyone's expense, and in the end is not funny.

Providence grants us very few geniuses and such a large percentage of them, like St. Paul, do such everlasting harm. It is really one of the cruelest tricks; to be so miserly in the number of geniuses and so lavish in their talent for evil.

But, of course, what could one expect of a man like Saul or Paul who was a fanatical nationalist and a zealous persecutor of heretics? His conversion on the road to Damascus was no conversion but simply a switching of sides, so it was of no real substance. It has happened many times to many people. In the Germany of the 1930s for instance, many Communists became Nazis (not just for the sake of expedience either). And in this country, some of the most serious Christians became Communists and later some of the disillusioned Communists became Catholics. It all amounts to the same thing: large, well-run organizations always give the appearance of being better run than they really are, and of being able to provide eternal shelter for anyone who is no longer amused or challenged by the changing unpredictable climate outisde.

This brings to mind a young Spanish woman I met in Paris, right after World War II. She was a refugee from Franco's Spain. She told me very seriously that Mary was her mother and that Karl Marx was her father. Thus this young woman provided herself with both shelters: the Catholic and the Marxist.

She told me that Mary and Marx were her personal guides and that each spoke to her directly. Discretion and a certain cowardice in my character forbade me from asking her in what language they addressed her. (Besides Spanish, she spoke French, Italian and English, so you see she was not entirely unprepared. However, ancient Aramaic and classical Latin are what I privately like to think they settled on).

In all of this, I do not mean to mock the Spanish young woman or Saul-Paul, apostle-tentmaker, converted-converter. I choose to mock no one. Our human need for shelter is all too obvious. Paul said many beautiful things along with some pretty atrocious stuff: "It is better to marry than to burn," he said—a genial concession to making love. The women's liberation stands on much solid ground. And the poor man had to suffer two years in a Roman prison for allegedly inciting a riot. And then, under the insane terror of Nero, he was probably beheaded. Yet what a lot of harm he did, after, as well as before his vision on the road to Damascus.

Enough of my jeremiads on the scarcity of genius and the perverse squandering of it. With just a little more modesty what a great deal less harm would be done.

N o, you do not have to be afraid to open this letter, but do not be too annoyed with me for not being jealous of you for falling in love with someone. (Drug addiction! draft difficulties! how that must appeal to the great mother in you.) I am pleased that he heard me speak once with Joan B. and was impressed.

Tell your Thomas Warner that I think him very lucky to have found you (or did you go looking for him?), and that all the lovely things you can do you learned from me (cooking and what not . . .)

No, just tell him that a middle-aged gentleman envies him a little more than is gentlemanly.

In a sense I've been waiting for this to happen (your having a lover your own age) since the day you arrived at college, which is in itself a form of jealousy. Please accept it as such, for I do feel somewhat remiss that I am not in a high dramatic rage, ready to fly across the continent to wrest you from the arms of my successor. Hollywood, if not all popular literature would at least have me get drunk, be maudlinly riotous in a brothel and reel into deserted night streets, cursing you and the universal whoredom of women, including the now standard wicked witch at the cradle, poor old Mom.

Can you envision my behaving this way?

Nor can I.

What does occur to me is a very funny remark of Graham Greene's: "God could not have been completely serious when he gave us genitals."

Darling, I know that you, who understand intuitively more than most people learn in a lifetime, know I am, in part, making fun of myself, you, and love relationships in general, in order to dilute my feelings and not cry here among all my books. But I want you to know, or rather I want to write it down plainly, because I am certain you already know, in spite of, or more likely because of my light tone, I love you tenderly, passionately and deeply.

And although I am suspicious of grandiose sentiments and words such as 'forever,' 'always,' 'eternal,' I would hazard a guess, a prediction: I shall love you tenderly, passionately and deeply as long as I live.

And although it is glorious to be loved, and for me inexpressibly glorious to have been loved by you, it is loving that is the supreme joy. It is loving that makes us no longer orphans on this earth. And it is only by loving that we put an end to the terrible anguish of loneliness and our measureless fear of death.

And for all this, which has not changed, which cannot change, I thank you with all my heart.

> "Let me not to the marriage of true minds
> Admit impediments. Love is not love
> Which alters when it alteration finds,
> Or bends with the remover to remove:
> O, no! It is an ever-fixed mark,
> That looks on tempests and is never shaken;
> It is the star to every wandering bark,
> Whose worth's unknown, although his height be taken.
> Love's not Time's fool, though rosy lips and cheeks
> Within his bending sickle's compass come;
> Love alters not with his brief hours and weeks,
> But bears it out even to the edge of doom.
>> If this be error, and upon me prov'd,
>> I never writ, nor any man ever lov'd."

Yes, of course, I will go on writing to you.

48

P

erhaps I would have felt better had I gone reeling into the streets inveighing curses against Mom and all of the rest of you. But I still don't really feel that way and I do understand. I shall just have to get used to the fact of you and Thomas.

Your letter doubtless is the reason for these lines to torment my consciousness this morning.

"At my back I always hear
Time's winged chariot hurrying near;
And yonder all before us lie
Deserts of vast eternity."

Marvel's piercing perfect arrow strikes dead center into the heart of all men for all times. Seventeenth century English poetry is unsurpassed. Begin with the *Oxford Book of 17th Century Verse,* by far the best book of that series, and read and re-read that always admirable George Herbert:

Mark you the floore? That square speckled stone,
    Which looks so firm and strong
        Is patience.

Herbert is right. The floor of all our activities is patience. Whether we like it or not, it is our greatest urgency.

Your college library should have volume two of *The English Poets-* edited by T. H. Ward- The 17th Century: Ben Johnson to Dryden. It was first published by MacMillan and Co. in 1880, and last reprinted, as far as I know, in 1912. By now there may be a current paperback edition of it in your local drugstore (one of the few mass-produced items that have my whole-hearted endorsement—paperback books, not drugstores.) This book, if anything, is more delightful than the Oxford book. Ward had a keen eye and a loving heart. Space, i.e. money, probably did not permit Ward or the editors of the Oxford book to include Milton's entire *Samson Agonistes.* My unqualified recommendation is that you read it all if you haven't already. I can literally see the look of surprise and wondrous pleasure in your eyes as you read it.

Milton, Marvel, Henry Vaughan, to name but three:

49

dreaded, hated, indigestible morsels for generations of school-children. Yet they gave such exquisite timeless gifts: a heady wine that never sours and never causes hangovers, the most refined sustenance that is at once simple fare and a magnificent banquet, never giving gout or going stale. Still, to imprisoned schoolchildren—a forced diet, horrible, tasteless, lumpy, disgusting stuff to be swallowed as quickly as possible. Smiling, poor children, when in truth they feel like wretching.

My God, schools and school teachers have a lot to answer for. In fact, this is not one of their minor crimes. It's a good thing I do not believe in the death penalty, because almost invariably, schoolmarms and schoolmen and school-boards are guilty of first degree murder: survey literature classes, classes in art and music appreciation . . . oh, dear, I forgot. One of these genteel handbills of shameless fraud is probably sitting in front of you on your desk at this moment: spring's latest list for the kidnapping of young minds.

As usual, this wasn't at all what I meant to write to you today. But oh, how much more enjoyable it would be if we were allowing ourselves to be educated while leisurely walking the streets of Florence, casually nodding to the Donatellos as we pass.

A volcano of irony has erupted; I cannot give it its due, cannot give it the demanding, immense proportions it deserves. An exuberance of ironies beyond all ironies! But I console myself (and it is no mean consolation) that no ironist, none at all, indeed not all of them working feverishly together, alive and dead, ancient and modern, east and west, could do justice to what has happened within the past week in this world of ours. No, on the contrary, it is not our world—its presiding spirit belongs to an incomprehensible and incomprehendable enigma of unparalleled immensity that has nothing, but absolutely nothing, to do with us. It is some fantastic comic spirit that goes infinitely beyond all fantasy, all comedy, all spirit. The closest perhaps, man has to suggest it is in the delightful, droll figure of the smiling Buddha. What the Buddha, the awakened one, is cheerfully smiling or laughing at we do not know, and we do not know if he knows.

What has happened during this past week could have been Gilbert and Sullivan's most marvelous parody, their most outrageously hilarious musical comedy. The audiences may have never been able to leave the theater, having literally drowned in the uncontrollable tears of their laughter.

And now after this elaborate introduction, I can no longer put off my puny offering.

After years of ugly and dangerous non-recognition, of ferocious and bellicose denunciations and accusations and of actual warfare in Korea in the 1950s, China and the United States of America have a more amicable political relationship. China graciously invited American ping pong players to come to its country, and the Americans graciously accepted.

What expert on Chinese American affairs would have, could have imagined it? None! But if there had been one somewhere that audacious, he would have been promptly laughed at, leaped upon, and locked up. It is true that during all these years, Chinese and American delegates have been meeting sporadically and unofficially in Poland, no doubt mutually agreeing, so neither would have an advantage, to

51

speak in Polish: a language neither of them would understand. But by God, no, they were playing ping pong the whole time.

When I read in the New York Times these recent inscrutable events I turned to Joseph Neeham's admirable and comprehensive volumes, *Science and Civilization in China.* In all of the scholarly and detailed indices there is not one reference to ping pong or, as it is known to the afficionados, table tennis. And here, in surely one of the most completely reliable and sympathetic sources available on China, is not a single entry on that humble game that may well have postponed the demise of the world.

Now who will dare, among all the noisy claimants, to boast that they and their group are the most politically relevant? Ping pong players of the world unite! The laurels are yours.

One last, lovely crowning note.

Who welcomed these youthful American invaders? No less a personage than Chou En-Lai, China's first minister. These happy North American barbarians met one of the most astute, interesting, resilient, sophisticated (no doubt ruthless when he deemed it necessary), and cultivated men of the world—the aristocratic mandarin turned communist.

My laughter would be unmarred were we not still killing each other all over the world.

I am delighted that you and Thomas Warner are getting on so well, that he is doing something about his heroin and draft problems, and that you have found a small house that is perfect for your needs: financially, utilitarianly and aesthetically. I am glad too that you have at last obtained what you for so long wanted, and what your consideration for my nasty allergy had kept you from having: two handsome Persian cats. I have never known why these elegant, intelligent creatures have always made me sneeze so preposterously. Surely one of the great disciples of the great Freud could reveal it to me after many years and thousands of dollars, but I shall continue to take the simpler, shorter, more cowardly and economic course of avoiding the little beasts (the Persian cats, of course, not the Freudians).

I'm flattered, I guess, that you named the male of the pair ofter me. But the name of the female is definitely beautiful, appropriate and in knowledgeable taste. Thomas could not have chosen better. It would seem that he and I have not a few things in common. Shirin was, as he probably told you, a beautiful Persian princess. It would be more fitting, though certainly I do not insist, that you change the male's name to that of Shirin's lover, Ferhad. For Ferhad exhibited an extraordinarily patient, cat-like quality by digging through a huge mountain in order to reach his princess.

The great 14th century (8th century of the Islamic era) Persian lyric poet Hafiz mentions them as he does many other fascinating things of his Sufi culture. You should read him (and there are now a number of good translations). His real name is Shams-ud-din. His short *nom de plume* of Hafiz literally means 'one who remembers,' which was applied (and perhaps still is) to any person who had learned the Koran by heart. He was one of those delightfully gifted poets who was also apparently, unabashedly a genuine mystic, scholar and rascal.

Listen love, if Thomas knows these things and tells them to you, let me know, so I bore you as little as possible.

At the risk of protesting too much, it does really please

me that things are going on well with you two. You are wise
enough to know that there will also be difficult times. If you
think I could be of any help, I am here. I listen well. I listen
particularly well to you.

Ira

Years ago, not so many really, in a small ramshackle town in Mississippi I was talking with Martin Luther King. Sadly, he was saying: "We find out about people, places, their history, condition, location and geography most often when some tragedy strikes them."

He was thinking primarily of the little town we were in, which most of us had not heard of until the day before. We had flown there, he—from Atlanta, Georgia, and I—from San Francisco, when we had learned that nine little black children (the oldest was ten years old) were severely beaten by a handful of grown white men as the children were walking to the town's first integrated school. Martin Luther King was also thinking of the new names of cities in Vietnam.

And today, like most days and nights, for all too many years, I think of the horrible war and the many names we have since become tragically familiar with in Vietnam, and really all over Indo-China.

Today, mass peaceful demonstrations against the war in Indo-China are scheduled to take place, principally in Washington and San Francisco. Undoubtedly you will be in the one in Washington as I will be in the one in San Francisco. (That is why I write you earlier in the morning than I generally do.) I am certain, too, that there will be smaller demonstrations in other American cities as well as in cities throughout the world. It is encouraging and significant that many of the people who will be taking part, will be doing so for the first time. This includes American soldiers, many of whom are Vietnam veterans.

To be opposed to this particular war has become downright respectable. Yet today numerous young men are serving relatively stiff prison sentences for their opposition to it and to military conscription.

It is at once heartening and discouraging. More and more people openly and actively find the Vietnam War (and at long last, war itself) unacceptable. Yet it continues. I am, however, more heartened than discouraged. But I am not an Indochinese, worried that my children, friends, neighbors or myself may at any moment be burned, bombed, or shot or have already suffered unspeakable losses of land, limbs, loves and lives. Nor am I some poor, bewildered, bamboozled, propagandized American boy-soldier in Vietnam, terrified that I will be blown to unrecognizable bits as so many others have.

And after six thousand years of organized warfare, which has done nothing but increase the sum of man's misery, we still mindlessly cling to that violence which we have yet to renounce for the utter failure that is is.

The Vietnamese themselves in recent past (I won't take you through the millenia of their heroic and tragic history) have been violently fighting foreign invaders since 1941. Thirty years! And one could legitimately go back at least another 33 years. But in 1941 Ho Chi Minh organized the Viet Minh—the league for the independence of Vietnam—to struggle against the occupation by the Japanese, who had driven out the French. Ho Chi Minh's first attempts to rid his country of the French were presumably in 1908, and he had many predecessors. In 1954, the French, after having settled in again at the end of WW2, were at last sent packing, being overwhelmingly defeated at Dien Bien Phu (see Jean LaCouture's excellent biography *Ho Chi Minh*, New York 1968).

How did America get involved in all this? I shall tell you without fail, at a later date. In the meantime, I shall put on my peace walking shoes and my body on a sunny Saturday line.

No, one more thing before I stop writing for today, because it is as important as it is psychologically alarming.

If the Vietnamese had been fighting nonviolently for these last thirty years, and the fighting was still going on, as it presently is, everyone would be saying: "You see, nonviolence is a failure. It doesn't work." Whereas no one, absolutely no one, not after thirty years, not after six thousand years, says organized violence is a failure; that it doesn't work.

The social and political organization of nonviolence, satyagraha, was first invented by Gandhi in South Africa, in 1906, only 65 years ago. People first said it was an impossibility, and then forty-one years later, when India won its independence from the British Empire, Gandhi and nonviolence were scarcely given credit.

The American scholar, George Sarton, did proclaim it "the greatest political event in the history of man." And Albert Einstein called Gandhi "a victorious fighter who always scorned the use of violence; a man who confronted the brutality of Europe with the dignity of a simple human being and thus at all times has risen superior."

When Martin Luther King began the American nonviolent movement by boycotting the segregated buses in Montgomery, Alabama, everyone said it could not be done. Yet when it was, the same critics said it was finished. When more and more was accomplished, they said it was of no importance, which absolutely was not true; it stirred the whole world. And when Martin Luther King was assassinated in 1968, 13 years after the Montgomery, Alabama boycott, the identical people who unremittently refused to acknowledge the birth of the nonviolent movement announced that it had died.

Let me assure you that nonviolence is not dead. On the contrary, it is growing: the draft resisters, the migrant farm workers and Cesar Chavez, the Sicilian peasants and Danilo Dolci.

Its old adversary, violence, though beloved by the media, is in its long overdue death agony. But nonviolence is here to stay and so are we. King said it neatly: "Nonviolence or nonexistence."

I must rush.

Ira

P.S. Read Peter Mathieson's book, *Sai Si Puedes*, it deals with Chavez and the nonviolent farmworkers in this country. Danilo Dolci, who is known as "the Gandhi of Sicily" has had five of his books translated into English. Read at least the last one, which is excellent, *The Man Who Plays Alone*.

Why have most people never heard of Dolci, but have of Che Guevara? Alas, we have yet to grow up. We still prefer the hero with the gun to the unarmed men of wisdom.

What with the peace march, large numbers of people, lighthearted spirits, dismal speeches and aching limbs—the weekend passed. So I will turn, as promised, to America's dreary, blood soaked, disreputable involvement in Vietnam.

Its origin is this country's real and manufactured fear of what is mystifyingly and vaguely summed up as communism.

I am in total agreement with the following comments of professor John King Fairbank of Harvard University:

"Our fear of communism," says professor Fairbank, "as partly an expression of our general fear of the future, will continue to inspire us to aggressive anti-communist policies in Asia and elsewhere. The American people will be led to think and may honestly believe that the support of anti-communist governments in Asia will somehow defend the American way of life. This line of American policy will lead to American aid to established regimes which attempt to suppress the popular movements in Indonesia, Indochina, the Philippines, and China . . . Thus after setting out to fight communism in Asia, the American people will be obliged in the end to fight the peoples of Asia."

These remarkably prescient comments were made in 1947, and are at once the background and prophecy of America's invasion of Vietnam. (Also see Fairbank's book, *The United States and China,* 3rd edition, Cambridge, Mass. 1971).

What Professor Fairbank saw happening in 1947 has gone on happening ever since.

In 1950, the United States, under the Democratic administration of Harry Truman, agreed to help France to finance its war in Vietnam. George Marshall was Secretary of Defense and Henry Stimpson, the Secretary of War—the last. After his resignation in 1945, we have only had Secretaries of Defense.

Indeed, war for glory and heroism is out. Noble defense is in. This "defense" is the euphemism for everyone's violence. Personal as well as collective, domestic as well as foreign. U.S. Marines use it, as do the Black Panthers.

58

The Deacons for Justice and Defense, for example, was the beginning of the end of the American nonviolent civil rights movement. (It was a self-appointed, armed group to protect civil rights workers, first in Louisiana). It's instructive to remember, too, that the Mafia was originally an armed organization to defend Sicilian peasants.

Maybe it is a good sign that war for glory is out of fashion. But "wars of liberation," of "self-determination" and "guerilla warfare" are still popularly heralded and the same old horrors go marching on.

To return to Vietnam. It was in 1953 that, under the Eisenhower administration, America's financial and moral pace really quickened. The aid increased progressively and enormously until it reached 785 million dollars, almost the entire cost of the French expeditionary force. Still, for the Vice President of the United States, Richard Milhous Nixon, the Quaker from California, this was not enough. He said: "If to avoid further communist expansion in Asia and Indochina we must take the risk of putting our boys in (his boys!) I think the executive has to take the politically unpopular decision and do it."

The formidable, religiously fanatical anti-communist Secretary of State John Foster Dulles fully agreed with him. Dulles, just for your information, was reputedly the highest paid lawyer in America. He was President of the World Council of Churches and a brother to the chief of the Central Intelligent Agency (CIA). A man, it would be safe to say, who had extraordinary connections; privy, no doubt, to all the secrets of this world and the next and zealously rushing us toward the latter. In those distant days of the fifties this was known as "brinkmanship."

There are still stories abroad that Nixon and Dulles wanted to use nuclear weapons to avoid France's defeat, but that Eisenhower would not consider it. If it is true, we must give a prayer of thanks to our late, golf-playing president. I wish all the presidents, prime ministers, dictators etc., would take up golf, cribbage, or something, and give up power politics.

In 1954, after the French defeat at Dien Bien Phu, an agreement was reached, temporarily partitioning Vietnam (North and South) along the 17th parallel until the time of general election, which was to be held no later than July, 1956, and was to lead to the reunification of the country. In the South, Bao Dai, emperor and a French collaborator was replaced and Dinh Diem, the American puppet was installed as the first Premier of South Vietnam, allegedly until reunification took place. At the same time, Ho Chi Minh formally took control of the North and the Viet Minh came to power. When this happened, more than 800 thousand Vietnamese, mostly Roman Catholics, began moving to the South—one of the many large, heart-breaking migrations of this century. These arbitrary military-political-economic divisions of countries have been unimaginably callous and cruel, taking everything into account except people. Obviously, to consider real, living people would be much too reactionary.

And on that uplifting thought I shall take leave and return to you and the Vietnamese story tomorrow.

I hope all continues to go well with you.

H

appily, deliberately, I'm not immediately resuming my grim chronicle of the Vietnam war. Why? My spirits are too good, too bouyant, too high.

It is now three a.m. I left my apartment at about four, yesterday afternoon and did not return until close to midnight. I did nothing special during the day; I spent the morning hours and the early afternoon ones, until I went out, reading and writing—the telephone securely caged, muzzled and muffled in the closet. (No, truthfully, it was artfully gagged.) One cannot be too cautious with this irritating, intrusive, ill-mannered beast which can be as colourfully camoflaged as a chameleon, whose shape can be protean and which can even take to making odious obscene simulations of chimes and cooing. If one keeps the beast on the premise at all, it must be strongmindedly dealt with. It is either you or it. And since 1876 it has been increasingly it.

And it was not, in reality, Alexander Graham Bell's fault, but his father's, Alexander Melville Bell. The old man taught elocution in London and worked out a system of "visible speech", a method of orthoepy in which the alphabetic characters of his own invention were graphic diagrams of positions and motions of the organs of speech. This enabled deaf mutes to learn to speak. And thus, it was only natural that little Alexander should develop an instrument for those of normal hearing so they could learn to speak like deaf mutes.

It was a very close, sensitive loyal family, even if in a bit of a rut; for the grandfather was another Alexander and was an authority on phonetics and defective speech.

You see, it would have been no morning for Vietnam. Although all the aforementioned facts are correct, I may be playing a little loose with the motives.

Well, to get on with my high spirits; after reading a new biography called *Gandhi in South Africa* and reworking an essay I wrote years ago as an introduction to Gandhi's own book, *Satyagraha in South Africa*, I visited my favorite bookstores and newsstands and bought a bunch of golden marigolds for the woman at the cleaners who faultlessly sewed a rip in my raincoat. I had supper and an evening of chamber music of Bartok and Bach at Stanford. Certainly that went on to sustain my high spirits.

My mood continues to be one of delight for no reason at all, or perhaps because it still holds the happy vision of the three generations of Alexander Bells commuting with triumphant Victorian probity from the laboratories and lecture halls of Edinburgh, London and Boston, dedicated, earnest and high-minded, but absolutely, phonologically, stark raving mad. All this while the world goes on tragically wounding and not so slowly killing itself, as the daily New York Times, with its amalgam of good taste and horror, continues to inform me.

This, then, is the appropriate place, before I forget it, to answer your question about which journals to read. I spend an hour each day doing it, as did my charmingly nagging, autocratic mentor, Mr. Gandhi. It is essential if you want to know what's going on. Actually I don't, but it is too irresponsible not to. I suppose one could, to a degree, substitute reliable television or radio news accounts for journalistic reading. But obstinate crank that you know I am, I've not let either of these abominations cross my threshold, although I know that occasionally illuminating things come from them.

The daily *New York Times* has an excellent news summary and Index. You could get away with reading just that, without even turning to the indicated pages, and you would be sufficiently informed of the world's up-to-date high and low doings. This is far and away the fastest, most painless way of getting the news, and sometimes, even authentically perceptive observations can be found. This may be just the thing for you with your much too crowded schedule. (Do not forget that school is an ancient Greek word, an ancient piece of wisdom, meaning leisure.)

Along with the New York Times you should subscribe to *I. F. Stone's Bi-Weekly.* (No, I shall send you a subscription to it.) Without question, I.F. Stone is one of the best journalists in the world. His small, generally four paged bi-weekly is a masterpiece of conciseness and information. Its value to its readers, even to those who have only heard it second hand, is immeasurable. Stone is irreplacable in a special way. Even when one disagrees with him (I think I scarcely would, were he a pacifist): his knowing pen carries integrity, autonomy, sanity and wit. In short, he is his own man and a fine one. I hope he lives forever in good working health. (After all, nature could make a few discriminating exceptions in the matter of mortality, or why could we not all be Endymions, the handsome shepherd lad to whom Zeus gave the two fold heavenly gift of eternal youth and of sleeping as long as he pleased.)

Anyway, I.F. Stone and The New York Times are the only required news reading. After that I would suggest your local newspaper, no matter how bad, so that you will know what is going on right outside you door.

The New York Review of Books is American culture, criticism, and politics at its best, although it too can be stuffy, inbred and tiresome, as all periodicals are at times.

Liberation Magazine, more or less new left, originally pacifist (although the New Left is now either dead or indistinguishable from the Old Left) is valuable primarily, but not only, because of Julius Lester's column, Aquarian Notebook. Julius Lester is a beautiful writer who gets better and better—see his book, *Search for the New Land*, New York, 1969.

Peace News, published in London, the only international nonviolent newspaper.

Win Magazine—East Coast, post hippie, pacifist, colourful and original.

Gentle Strength—the West Coast Win.

The Catholic Worker—25 cents a year. Mostly monthly, sometimes bi-monthly. It was co-founded and is presently edited by a woman named Dorothy Day. She has a moving autobiography, *The Long Loneliness*, now out of print, but libraries should have it.

Dorothy Day is a great woman. I visited with her recently in New York City. While talking with her, I was reminded of what the late Pope John 23 said when he was dying. He was asked if everything was as satisfactory as it could be considering the circumstances. He smiled and said: "All my bags are packed."

Dorothy Day gave the impression of a woman who had all her bags packed. Not that she seemed in the least danger of dying. On the contrary, at seventy three or four, she is excitingly alive. It is just abundantly clear that no matter what, no matter where, she was ready to go or stay. Simply ready, no matter what life demanded of her. Her newspaper is, as the name announces, labor and Catholic; it is also pacifist, communitarian, anarchist, and unbelievably harmonious.

The Monthly Review—a scholarly, interesting, non-communist, Marxist journal, which I sometimes feel (probably unfairly and unkindly) has a certain, irrepressible predilection for the jugular.

The Soviet Life and the *Peking Review*: so you can read their propaganda about our propaganda about their propaganda.

The Black Panther paper—in my opinion, no longer politically important, but emotionally significant.

The Berkeley Barb—so you have a notion of the style of the so-called underground press which disappointingly turns out to be as uniform and untrustworthy as the conventional press.

Move now to the "liberal" from the "radical"; terms that are, in the last analysis, a little to facile, yet will remain here with the understanding that they are a rough and unsatisfactory shorthand.

Commentary: Jewish, intelligent, and with some things one cannot find from any other source.

Commonweal: Catholic, intelligent, and with some things one cannot find from any other source.

Christian Century: Protestant, and has the same qualities of the two preceding.

Ebony: A magazine written for and by middle class blacks; it has a large circulation and like its late counterpart *Life*, is sometimes of real interest.

Time Magazine should be read if only to read the news magazine probably most people in the world are reading. Also, its coverage is good and has become, since the death in 1967 of its owner and editor-in-chief Henry Luce, considerably less obnoxious.

On the intellectual right is the National Review. It should be looked at now and again. It is not very engaging, but makes serious sophomoric efforts to be so.

64

Going across the Atlantic:

Le Monde in Paris is possibly the best daily newspaper in the world. Reading it would also keep your French brisk. Le Monde does have a weekly English edition as well.

The London Times is a little too self-consciously weighty, but it is important, dealing with events in Africa which are too often ommitted from the American press.

The London Observer has fine political, historical and cultural pieces. In a way, the New York Review of Books is its American equivalent.

There are good general scientific magazines: the *Scientific American*, the *Bulletin of Atomic Scientists*, *Science*, and *Nature*. And there are highly specialized journals in all fields. I could literally go on, but I will stop now for your sake, and mine.

You are my favorite labor of love; and coming very close to the sentencious, I will add: love sweetens the labor, as the labor deepens the love.

P.S. It just occurred to me that I left out one of the most interesting, varied, and curious encyclopedic magazines in America: *Manas*. Read it and tell all your friends about it. Its editor, Henry Geiger, is a man of great and unusual learning.

Do you take notes in class? The great 18th century German philosopher Emanuel Kant (he lived 4 years into the 19th century) strongly disapproved of the practice. He wanted his students to think for themselves and not become skilled imitators. It has been said that though he was humorous in the dry British manner, he was very easily distracted while lecturing. A button missing from a student's coat, a visible yawn, and he'd lose track of what he was saying. Once when several students were diligently writing down his every word with their quill pens he said: "Gentlemen, do not scratch so, I am no oracle." I do not think he would like the smooth whirring of tape recorders any better.

Kant was a tiny man, barely five feet tall, who dressed elegantly. Out of doors in good weather, he held a three cornered hat under his arm and sported a gold-headed cane.

Every afternoon at precisely the same time, rain or shine, he would take an hour's walk, never more, never less. He always took the same route along the Linden Allee of his city of Konigsberg.

When it was raining he carried a fine, huge old umbrella. If it only looked as if it were going to rain, a servant would walk behind him carrying the umbrella. Having the servant walk behind was not snobbery. His purpose was to walk alone. He felt it essential when outside to breath only through his nose, or risk catching cold. If he had a companion at his side, good manners would compel him to open his mouth and speak.

Twice, to the astonishment of the citizens of Konigsberg, he varied his immutable ways. Once he stayed inside for three consecutive days. He had been sent from Paris a copy of Rousseau's book *Emile*, and he almost literally could not put it down till he had finished it. The other time his alarmed, gaping neighbors saw him not walking down the Linden Allee, but along a different route. They knew something earthshaking must have happened. And they were not mistaken. He had just received the news of the beginning of the French Revolution.

What follows is not a précis in any sense, or an

oversimplification (you get enough of that at college) of Kant's large influential work. Much of his formal idealism is now widely and correctly (in my opinion) discredited, chiefly because his fundamental principles of God, ethical freedom of the will, and immortality, have not borne the weight of critical thought. Nevertheless, these are a few of his ideas that appeal to me and I think will always be valid:

Kant felt that education should not adapt itself to conditions of the world but should attempt to improve them substantially.

"Parents," he wrote, "usually educated their children merely in such a manner that however bad the world may be, they may adapt themselves to its present conditions. But they ought to give them an education so much better than this, that a better condition of things may thereby be brought about in the future."

In general, a little crudely and rudely perhaps, this is precisely the kind of education that children are presently giving their parents.

I have always had a warm spot in my heart for Kant, who spoke of the categorical imperative. "Act in such a way that you use human nature both in your own person and everyone else's always as an end, never merely as a means."

He also wrote an essay entitled "Perpetual Peace" in which he said: "Politics in the real sense cannot take a step forward without paying homage to the principles of morals."

P.S. The ancient walled city of Konigsberg where Kant lived and taught no longer exists. It was badly damaged during World War 2, and in 1945 was transferred to the Soviet Union. Its name is now Kaliningrad, and almost all of its inhabitants are Russian. I do not know if the statue of Kant, which was the pride of the city, still stands. I like to think that it does.

*Early to
Mid May
1971*

I do not know what it is, but by something I do or do not do, I continually offend Somnus, the god of sleep, not to be confused with Morpheus, the god of dreams. My nightly offering, placed on the immaculate alter of devoutly prepared darkened stillness is left untouched. Perhaps there should be one votary candle aglow? Is my silence too haughty? my meditations too trite? my incantations too worn? He deigns not enter my unholy chambers, this illusive god.

Perhaps my decade of false and wanton worship of his shadow pretender, the evil barbituate, remains unforgiven. Well, whatever, I fervently hope that Mr. Shelley, blessed of poetry and twice cursed with drowning (his young and beautiful wife Harriet's deliberately, followed six years later by his own, accidentally); yes, I hope he was wrong in his poem "Mont Blanc" when he wrote:

"That death is slumber,
and that it shapes the busy thoughts
outnumber,
Of those who wake and live."

Good Lord! That would be the ultimate humorless practical joke; not to be able to sleep peacefully even then. But the god of Auschwitz, nerve gas and napalm must never, never, as all theologians agree, be thought of as having limitations.

And this, after a pleasant lapse of several days, brings us back to the squalid story of Vietnam.

On this very day one American young man (white) in one kind of uniform (a civilian's) stabbed to death another American young man (black) in a different kind of uniform (a soldier's). I heard people say: "How can such terrible things happen?"

And they are right. It is terrible. But my question is why is it not happening more often in a world maddened by war, saturated with fears, and stupefied by hate? It is something of a miracle that someone isn't cutting his own throat or someone else's every moment. But, then, how do I know they are not?

In the atmosphere in which we are living, the killing of

71

that young soldier at his desk in the recruiting office was not an unusual event; no more an unusual event than the killing of Malcolm X, Martin Luther King, Medgar Evers, John Kennedy, Robert Kennedy, Lincoln Rockwell and all the names and nameless in Indochina: the Vietnamese, Americans, Koreans, Laotians, Cambodians and Thais. And I could include almost every other place in the world. According to the New York Times of June 1, 1970, "It is estimated that, in the course of the last decade, about 700,000 persons were killed during China's internal struggles; 500,000 died as a result of the Indonesian massacres; and 250,000 lost their lives during the civil war between Nigeria and Biafra. In Vietnam, 42,000 Americans have been killed, along with 110,000 South Vietnamese and 650,000 North Vietnamese. To these figures must be added those of the deaths in the Algerian war of 1960-1962 and in the Middle Eastern conflicts. Altogether, the number of people killed in this period of "peace" is roughly equal to the number of dead during the First World War."

The largest slaughter has taken place in China, but the victims were Orientals, so we care very little. Our real sorrow is sorrowfully selective. My God! It is no wonder that Quincy Wright's book, *A Study of War* (revised edition, Chicago, 1965) runs to 1,637 pages. And its brevity, I'm sure, is due simply to fatigue.

Doubtless the time of death occurs for someone somewhere every moment. But it need not ever be caused by murder; not by knife, bullet, bomb, hunger, or the bite of a rat in a tenement.

In our Vietnam chronicles we left over eight hundred thousand predominantly Roman Catholic Vietnamese making their way south as Ho Chi Minh took formal control of North Vietnam. This was in 1954. (I'm going to give you just the skeleton—hideously apposite figure of speech—of the central facts of the war so I can bring you quickly up to date.)

In 1955, the MAAG, United States 'Military Assistance Advisory Group' began training the South Vietnamese army. The press soon referred to MAAG simply as advisors.

According to the Geneva agreement, talks were to begin

in preparation for the election in the following year. However, Diem, Premier of South Vietnam, instructed by the Americans, refused to accept North Vietnam's invitation to these talks. Then Diem became South Vietnam's first President of the Republic, by defeating Bao Dai in a conveniently limited referendum. Bao Dai returned to his beloved French Riviera; that is where he was when most of the nasty fighting was going on in Vietnam. The patriotic Diem spent most of that time in the United States. Their distant residences during this period, as you can imagine, won them the hearts of the people (the French and the American).

As you can guess, or already know, in 1956, in spite of the Geneva agreement, the United States refused to permit elections to take place on the grounds that the elections would not be honest, which meant, as everyone knew and as Eisenhower wrote, that Ho Chi Minh would win in any free, fair, open, national elections.

From 1957 through 1960, the repression was on and insurgency followed. The MAAG was increased from 327 to 685. The coalition, communist-led National Liberation Front (NLF) was founded in South Vietnam, and the Viet Cong replaced the Viet Minh, many of the same people, of course, simply adopting the change in the name of the organization as they came out of brief retirement.

In 1961, the liberal, engaging, peace-loving, handsome young American president, John Fitzgerald Kennedy, created the Green Berets, "several hundred specialists in guerilla warfare to train Vietnamese soldiers," and the United States openly allowed their counterinsurgency program to be known. By the end of the year there were 3200 advisors.

All this time, no, since 1955 through the present, the American government has assured and assured the American people that the war was, is and has always been going well for the South Vietnamese. Fewer and fewer Americans believe it. Outside of this country, no one believes it.

In 1962, a United States Military Assistance Command was established in Saigon, headed by a four-star general, Gen. Paul Harkins. Diem, his brother, and his beautiful and powerful bitch of a sister-in-law, Madame Nhu, made the regime day by day more autocratic, corrupt and unpopular.

The fact that they were a family of Catholics in this Buddhist country added a further alien cast to their government. The Catholic church and Western domination had long been imperious, imperial and inseparable.

In 1963 there were large Buddhist demonstrations against the regime in Saigon and Hue, and they were savagely crushed. In an incredibly heroic protest, between June and October, seven Buddhist monks burned themselves to death. (My heart, my admiration and my disapproval accompany such acts which have tragically inspired others to do the same in this country and in France, as well as in Vietnam).

In November there was a Vietnamese military coup (certainly with the knowledge and assistance of the Americans) overthrowing the Diem government. Diem and his brother were murdered, but Madame Nhu escaped. After Diem's assassination there were ten successive governments in the next 18 months.

I am glad that Madame Nhu escaped, ghastly woman that she is. Anyone's murder, for any reason, is a tragedy in itself and prepares the ground for another murder and another and another.

Everyone knows we imitate what is done, not why we say it is done. It is the act that teaches, not its justification.

I'm going to go on with this horror story, but I would suggest that you stop reading now (if you haven't already) and come back to it tomorrow. If you break off now, know that my love goes with you.

In the exact same month of November, John Kennedy was murdered in Dallas, Texas.

"Do not send to know for whom the bell tolls. It tolls for thee." John Donne wrote that five centuries ago. How much longer is that going to take us to learn? How many more centuries, how many more murders?

In 1964, General Wm. Westmoreland became the American commander in South Vietnam. It was the year of the Gulf of Tonkin hoax. Two American destroyers were allegedly attacked by North Vietnamese torpedo boats. Congress passed a resolution in the best language of governmental duplicity that empowered Lyndon Baines Johnson to "repel any armed attack against the forces of the United States to prevent further aggression."

74

It was Johnson's carte blanche. It was his Green Berets. He had equalled if not surpassed John Kennedy.

In February of 1965 after (of course) the Viet Cong attacked a United States outpost at a place called Pleiku, and when United States dependents were evacuated from South Vietnam, American bombers began systematic raids over North Veitnam. But it was not until June of that year that the Americans *for the first time* admitted that twenty-three thousand of their "advisors" were involved in direct combat. And before the end of the year America had sent in more than 150,000 troops.

In 1966-67 the war continued to increase with more and more deaths (body counts, as they are called with the most tasteless and sterile barbarity) and at last, protest against the war began to grow and gain more attention in the United States.

In 1968 the National Liberation Front mounted its first huge Tet offensive (the lunar new year). General Westmoreland asked for and was duly delivered two hundred and six thousand more lives (troops, young men with heartbeats, longings, confusions and foot lockers).

In March, President Johnson unexpectedly and spectacularly announced that he was withdrawing as a presidential candidate. The anti-war movement gets credit for it, but, alas, we have not yet stopped the war. Nevertheless, it was nice to see Johnson go, but particularly disagreeable to see Nixon arrive. At the same time a defeated Vietnamese peace candidate in Saigon was imprisoned for five years for "actions harmful to the anti-communist spirit of the people and the army."

A General Abrams replaced General Westmoreland, who then at a press conference said that the Vietnam war would not end in a military victory. I think he was the first American official to say what the man on the street had been saying for years. And because of widespread demonstrations, long days and sleepless nights, the bombing of North Vietnam was stopped and preliminary peace talks began in Paris.

And thanks to many events in 1968, not the least of which was the vulgarity and ugliness in Chicago, centering around the Democratic convention, in January, 1969, with strenuous work done on all sides, the country moved a little to the right and inaugurated Richard Milhous Nixon president, pleasing both the conservatives and the indomitable, die-hard, it-will-hasten-the-revolution extreme left primitives.

In 1970 Ho Chi Minh died and America invaded Cambodia. But there was such immediate and vigorous protest that Mr. Nixon had the troops removed quickly and sent them to sorely offending, relentlessly aggressive Laos. And all the time, especially now, in 1971, the American government tells of its troop withdrawals and the "winding down" of the war in that inscrutable Occidental manner of carrying it into three countries instead of one. To us commonplace people of the world it may look as if America were widening the war; that is only because we are becoming cynical and do not understand the majestic and esoteric maneuvers of our venerable statesmen.

My love, I know how much you must have regretted my omission of the 1968 My Lai massacre. It and its repercussions have been so odd, I am saving them for a special letter. I know you can scarcely wait, nor can I.

Even through all this muck and murder, this letter carries my love.

On Sundays I miss you more than on any other day of the week. This day has a peculiar, pensive, heavy, oppressive air like a sailing ship becalmed. Henry James, better than anyone, described the distinctly repellent ambiance of Sundays in his novel *Princess Cassimasima.*

I would like to be surprised by your knocking on my apartment door, now that, with a proper ceremonial note, you have mailed back my keys.

It was curious and mildly disturbing that in the same note you said you and Thomas were not getting on as well as before. It almost sounded as if, at least for the moment, you would have liked to return Thomas' keys, too.

I recognize the familiar, vague, uneasy tone you get when something is going wrong and you can't put your finger on it. But your record should give you reason for optimism. In the past, your troubling, haunting uneasiness always showed itself, exorcised itself, or just happily vanished. This will undoubtedly happen again. Patience, my love, patience. (Always the easiest advice from the distant sage who is not enjoined to carry it out or suffer what is being suffered).

Damn, what a dreary subject. And today I was going to write to you a light letter to balance yesterday's sheet of human squalor. But the Sunday staleness stole into my apartment like a priest in mufti. And I have a feeling of sermons and shawls and prayer books; a million people down on their knees—all on my chest.

> "I will arise and go now, and go to Innisfree
> And a small cabin build there of clay and wattles made;
> Nine bean rows will I have there,
>   a hive for the honey bee,
> And live alone in the bee-loud glade,
> And I shall have peace there, for peace comes dropping
>   slow,
> Dropping from the vales of the morning to where the
>   cricket sings;
> There midnight's all a-glimmer, and noon a purple glow,
> And evening full of the linnet's wings.

77

That's W. B. Yeats and it's beautiful, and the old Irish magician has made me feel better already. How can one stay gloomy when there are such lovely things at hand? One cannot, unless one nourishes and sustains a great breast-beating, or a sulky introverted temperament. Then perhaps if we don't get the gloom we deserve, we at least get the gloom we desire. Seek ye first the kingdom of self-pity and its righteousness and all these things shall be added unto thee.

I shall arise now and stop playing a Sunday morning Kafka. I shall take a walk in the fresh green hills behind Stanford University, which for some reason reminds me that yesterday in my preoccupation with the chronicles of the Vietnam war, I forgot to wish you a happy May Day.

Happy May Day, love. I hope it's fine for you and Thomas in the spring beauty of New England (spring is not so bad in old England either).

In ancient India and Egypt, fertility festivals would be celebrated, and considering these countries today no one could accuse these particular deities of witholding their favors.

In ancient Rome, we'd have brought garlands to the goddess Flora, and in medieval England, with gay streamers flying, we would have danced merrily around the maypole. And in 1889, had we been members of the second Socialist International, we would have declared the first day of May an annual holiday for radical labor to take to the streets and show burger and nobility we were alive and on the move.

I'm on the move to the hills.

M

y walk in the hills yesterday amid fresh grass, the pastel lavender of lupin, and the flaming orange of the wild California poppy, was cut short by a sudden downpour. Had I been properly prepared for it (like Kant with my servant carrying a large umbrella) I would not have hurried for shelter, as I much like walking in the rain. But I had blithely worn the lightest of clothes and had not even bothered to take a jacket.

I happily spent the rest of the afternoon in the three bookstores in the area that are open on Sunday. As usual, I purchased a number of books. My real lack of interest in other things except for original paintings, drawings and sketches, most of which I cannot begin to afford, generally leaves me with sufficient funds for books. And as you know (do you know everything about me or nothing? The latter would come closest to my own knowledge of myself) I very seldom add to my stock of records, simply because over the years I have gotten most of the things I like to listen to.

I also know you know I'm putting off trying to give you advice about your difficulty with Thomas even though you have unequivocally requested it. I feel it puts me on a specially vertiginous and potentially treacherous tightrope.

I am, first of all, *a priori,* suspicious of all advice. But in this matter I also start off being profoundly suspicious of myself. The last sentence for instance; it appears so reasonable, generous, scrupulous and humble. And yet I possess none of these qualities, or such a small amount of each. God, what nonsense! You can, I suppose, be a little generous, but certainly not a little scrupulous nor a little humble. Either you are these things or you are not. And definitely I am not either of them (especially in relationship to you). I genuinely think (although Paul Valerie is right: "consciousness reigns, but does not govern") that above all I wish for your happiness. But, having a passing acquaintance with the writer of these lines, I don't believe it for one moment. In my heart of hearts, in the recesses of my mind, I would guess that I would subordinate your happiness to mine. And that means, darling, I would not be displeased if your troubles with

Thomas culminated in a final breach and you returned to me.

So *bon courage, bon chance*. But no advice; mouth closed, lips sealed.

And for God's sake, don't be taken in by my candor; it is the cleverest and most seductive trick of all. Candor and honesty do not in any fashion alter, modify, dissolve or excuse low motives, feelings or actions, as some seem to think. Their only value is that they could serve as a warning, but like advice, they are seldom accepted.

I t is five thirty in the morning; dark yet, and very still, save for the birds singing and my writing. But because I write not on a typewriter nor with a quill pen, but with an instrument not so archaic as the latter but almost as obsolete: the fountain pen, the sound I produce is considerably less than that of the birds.

The fine mingling and changing of color—black, violet and blue with a thin scattering of lamps and stars, framed by the sliding glass doors of the apartment, makes a superb backdrop for the invisible birds' joyous *matins*.

> Quick, said the bird, find them, find them,
> Round the corner, through the first gate,
> Into our first world, shall we follow
> The deception of the thrush? Into our first world.
> Go, said the bird, for the leaves were full of children,
> Hidden excitedly, containing laughter.
> Go, go, go, said the bird: human kind
> Cannot bear very much reality.

Well, inasmuch as you save all of my letters, I suspect that if you rearrange them with your offensively superior anagramatic skill, you would have T. S. Eliot's "Four Quartets" in its entirety.

I would suggest obtaining the record of Eliot's reading it: Angel Records; 45012. It makes one's own reading easier and more interesting. Most poetry should be read aloud, even when one is by oneself; too much is missed otherwise. I would recommend this for great prose, too; especially stories. Why rob ourselves unnecessarily of this integral, powerful, and beautiful element of language? It could help remind us of the extraordinary richness and subtle grandeur of our most important everyday tool, to which we are often much too indifferent.

But it's interesting, isn't it, that such is the force of conventional habit that we are embarrassed or taken aback or regard ourselves as a little loony if, alone, we suddenly become aware that we are spontaneously reading aloud? And we, at times, consciously inhibit ourselves from doing it. Who do we think is listening? Why do we assume that our unseen neighbor may not find it as beautiful as we do ourselves? And besides, what does it matter?

We are a loony species, but not without fascination, and I could be content with my *weitanschauung* (it means 'world-view,' sounds more impressive in German) of thoroughly amused irony, if we could but put an end to all the hideous unnecessary suffering. Then it would almost be pure comedy. No, I take it back. We would still have with us disease (hopefully less and less), death, heartbreaks, and natural disasters. That should be enough for the most insatiable sadist among us who could have his fill without a single war, without the subtlest political, economic, social or psychological tyranny. Surely in this, the Lord is his shepherd, he shall not want.

P.S. I shall send you the T.S. Eliot recording. It is one of my not insignificant joys: you, T.S. Eliot, and giving gifts. That reminds me, you should be receiving I. F. Stone's Bi-Weekly very soon. A friend told me that a university recently honored Stone for his great work in journalism, clear both to the intellectual and to the harried man on the street. It made me happy. Direct appreciation of the living makes much more sense than euologzing the dead.

It is a grey, chilly, moist morning. Spring is coming late to California. I am writing in a blue dressing gown, with the heat turned on.

There is a funny story connected with the dressing gown:

One afternoon while I was buttoning my suitably old faded workshirt in preparation for spending a few days with the farm workers in Delano, California, a merchant's delivery man came to the door. He handed me a package from Paris. Unlike Kant's gift of Rousseau's *Emile,* it came from Christian Dior. A French friend of mine sent me a simple (that elegant simplicity that only the rich can afford) plain, blue silk dressing gown. (Forgive me for the repeated use of the affected word 'dressing gown,' but bathrobe just would not do for this regal silk).

I let loose a real belly laugh, for I knew that that night I would be sleeping on the floor in a sleeping bag in another friend's not unpleasant tiny wooden cabin.

The timing of the arrival of the gift was perfect. The extremes of my life greeted each other in that precision of contradictions which I have always found irresistably comic: Gandhi in the best of Bond Street, which he actually wore as a young law student in London; and the fashionable King Edward the VIII in a loincloth—which alas never happened, not even in the many marvelous caricatures of him.

Gandhi was the greater aristocrat, nobility springing largely from his nature, whereas Edward's was, poor man, from his oppressive nurture. Do not forget, he was Queen Victoria's eldest son, and she was by most accounts, as dull as she was dogged, and queen she was for 64 eyars. Edward did not become king until he was 60.

Yet in spite of the immense difference between Gandhi and Edward VIII in style, character and condition, they had one rare and important attribute in common: each possessed an irrepressible gaity that neither age nor circumstance dulled. Victoria and Albert had done their rigid royal worst. And for Gandhi there had been prisons and fasts and disappointments. But bounce these two men had, and a merry mischievousness that arose in most unexpected places and kept them out of every quagmire.

You also have these delightful characteristics, though I know at the moment they are in abeyance, and I know too that when you feel as low as you do now, you think that it will never change, certainly never get better.

I promise you that it will.

I am glad, of course, that you are writing so often, though I am sorry that the reason is your depression; your troubles with Thomas. Or am I sorry? Well, I will not go on belaboring the point; I will assume that I am sorry. Generous assumptions are always in order even when the facts seem to indicate otherwise.

Love, you have persisted so tenaciously, so appealingly that, against my better judgment, I am, with reluctance, going to hazard some advice. And to show you what a cautious man I am, not to mention cowardly, I, who generally throw away your letters or anyone else's after I've answered them, have saved every one of yours in which you have pleaded for advice. I have had them notarized, xeroxed, microfilmed, and sent to safe deposit vaults in banks in all 22 cantons of Switzerland. The banks here have become too vulnerable, fiscally and politically. I have only taken this simple precaution for the day you rage at me for having made the whole thing up. One more word to delay a moment longer, if it is a mistake to seek advice of a former lover about a current love, and a greater mistake to give that advice, the greatest mistake of all would be to follow it.

All right, here it is: leave Thomas for a set period of time (mutually agreed upon) and no matter how much you miss each other, do not return earlier; or, on the other hand, do not stay longer than planned. Everyone needs a holiday from those he lives close to; everyone needs a holiday from himself, a holiday from that nauseating, narrow, internal self-centeredness.

And yet most of the holidays from ourselves are failures, end in disaster, and our last state is worse than the first.

A holiday is really precisely what it says (some of us take words too seriously, some—not seriously enough). It is a holy day; a day of holiness, which is a day of wholeness and health. The words are an indivisible, etymological trinity.

The attempted age-old holidays from oneself are: booze,

84

dope, and sex, and they doubtlessly go back to a trackless antiquity. And of course there is an infinity of variations, depending on character, conduct, circumstance and convenience. And despite their weighty lineage and world-wide usage, booze, dope and sex and all the other distractions are a tried and false and ruinous method of taking that long overdue holiday from oneself. But why one persists is obvious: even though these are bottomlessly stupid and apparently increase one's addiction, they do, in the short run, work.

> Distracted from distraction by distraction
> Filled with fancies and empty of meaning
> Tumid apathy but no concentration
> Men and bits of paper, whirled by the cold wind
> That blows before and after time . . .

In the long run, in the very nature of things, the distractions cannot work, cannot be helpful.

Knowing what the word means is useful. To distract is to draw or pull apart, so if healthiness is wholeness, distractions can only destroy our health.

Then is my suggestion to you of temporarily leaving Thomas not just another distraction? The famous running-away distraction? It certainly could be. We can, and generally do turn everything, from the lowest to the loftiest, into a series of distractions. Pascal thought we should be pitied more for the superficial quality of our distraction than for our real sufferings. But my advice to leave was not to help you run away, but hopefully to give you and Thomas more psychological space to breathe in, to be able to pay closer attention. To what? To everything. Paying attention is the opposite of distracting oneself. It is the medicine, my love, not bitter, but difficult to swallow, that if taken daily during every waking hour for the rest of our lives, will make us and keep us whole, healthy and happy.

I'm a little shy of holiness, but not of unconscionably long letters. But you have asked for it! And do not forget that I have proof of it in all 22 cantons of Switzerland, and I shall further confess that I have also given it to a nameless itinerant Tibetan monk who is in his 804th incarnation.

P.S. And this, I trust, will give you a certain pause when you again think of asking me for advice.

As easily predicted, I had not been able to write to you for the last two days, my time and energy having been spent in preparing for and talking with over 3000 high school students in Oakland, California.

I spoke formally to two large assemblies, informally in several classrooms, still more informally with individual students, teachers and administrators. It all went well, which means, by and large, I spoke with people rather than to them.

I received many compliments too generous to take seriously or to repeat. For whatever peculiar reason within myself, I was most encouraged by the fact that the best questions and comments as well as by far the most frequent ones came from black students. I can report with joy that Martin Luther King is not dead in their minds and hearts.

I will, I promise once again, tell you of some of the more interesting times I spent with King, especially now as you're embarking on a paper on him for sociology (it is a good idea to go into some African history as a background). I will try to tell you of incidents that you will not find in your library.

Needless to tell you, but brazenly I shall, for always, with seemingly unwearying kindness, you have allowed me to say things when you knew what I was going to say, but also how eagerly I wanted to say them.

Yesterday I spoke of many things, hopefully touching directly and not abstractly on the lives of all of us who were there. What I had to say radiated from Gandhi's *satyagraha*. Though it is still too difficult (at least for me) to use a sanskrit word gracefully and unaffectedly with a Western audience, *satyagraha* is now included, albeit inadequately defined, in both the *Webster's Unabridged Dictionary* and the *Unabridged Oxford English Dictionary*. The latter is affectionately known as the OED, and I do mean affectionately. I have great affection for each of the thirteen volumes' careful, unpedantic, fascinating scholarship. That and the 11th edition of the *Encyclopedia Britannica,* published in 1911, with a three volume supplement, constitute some of my most enchanting reading.

The combined forty five volumes of the Britannica and

the OED are on the bookshelf above my bed. So if California should have one of its much speculated upon earthquakes and I am in bed, I should be spontaneously given a most appropriate burial.

If you still have some good will left after making your way or skimming through my digressions, I will go on to say that instead of using the word *satyagraha* in public addresses, I talk of revolutionary nonviolence, expressing it thus:

It makes no sense to talk of nonviolence without revolution because nonviolence is the most active and complete principle and methodology of social change; and it is absurd to talk of revolution without nonviolence because all violence is reactionary, creating the exact conditions it intends to destroy.

We get what we do; not what we intend, not what we wish, not what we hope, but simply what we do. I have said it before and I shall say it again because it cannot be emphasized enough. Nonetheless you would think that after six thousand years of socially organized violence (war) and the present state of the world, it would be perfectly clear. But, alas, it is not. Not yet.

The human revolution is the insistance, in every sphere, on the sanctity and dignity of all human life; that all human life takes precedence over any idea of human life; that we develop ourselves and all institutions to help us care and share with all the people of the world and to resist any action, any organization, that would kill, injure, or diminish in any manner a single human being.

Armed resistance to tyranny has been and continues to be used by good men and women everywhere because they have not known any other way or have not been convincingly shown the effective alternative of revolutionary nonviolence, which is partially the failure of men like myself. Nevertheless, there can be no resistance to tyranny by arms or any form of violence. Armed resistance is a contradiction, it turns out to be no resistance at all, but the confirmation of tyranny. On the other hand, doing nothing, merely standing by, which is pathetic, which armed resistance is not, is, like secrecy, one of the most widely practiced and vicious species of violence and therefore has absolutely no connection to revolutionary nonviolence.

88

This, then, is the revolution, and it is love.

When I had finished speaking at the Oakland High School, the teacher who was my host thanked me and said: "You know, last year you would not have been permitted to speak at this school, and who knows, maybe next year they won't let you. But you are here today and we are all glad."

I shall close with an irresistable piece of immodesty. The youngsters gave me a very moving standing ovation.

Really, we all believe in love, we are just afraid to practice it.

J eremiah, chronically embittered by the desert, piteously
wailed:

"For this, gird you with sackcloth, lament and
howl . . . make ye mention to the nations, publish" against
America, that watchers come from a far country and give out
their voice against our cities . . . destruction upon destruction is cried; for the whole land is spoiled, it is Mother's Day!

It is the national tribute to Freud, Sophocles, and
commercialism. At the time of this great religious holiday the
devout should be making their pilgrimage to the shrines and
alters of Las Vegas and Miami Beach, Florida. For these
cities are sacred to the incomparable goddess of vulgarity.
Here for this occasion, as the psalmist tells us, "The words of
our mouths and the meditation of our hearts will be the most
acceptable in her sight." Unable to make this ritually
purifying journey, I have, instead, fortuitously recalled an
essay by Aldous Huxley entitled "Mother". It is to be found
in his book *Tomorrow and Tomorrow and Tomorrow*. It is
so outrageously good I am going to quote from it liberally.

"The family is an institution" he writes, "which permits
and indeed encourages the generation of immense quantities
of psychological energy. But until very recent times, this
energy was allowed to run to waste without doing any good
to industry or commerce. This was a situation which, in a
civilization dependent for its very existence on mass produc-
tion and mass consumption, could not be tolerated. The
psychological engineers got to work and soon the private,
random and gratuitous sentiments of filial devotion were
standardized and turned to economic advantage. Mother's
Day and Father's Day (despite the growing absurdity of Poor
Papa), were instituted, and it began to be mandatory for
children to celebrate these festivals by buying presents for
their parents, or at least by sending them a greeting card. Not
a letter, mind you; letters are private, random, and bring
money only to the post office. Besides, in these days of tele-
phones and progressive methods of teaching orthography,
few people are willing to write or able to spell. For the good
of all concerned (except perhaps the recipients, who might

have liked an occasional handwritten note), the greeting card was invented and marketed . . .

"Each of these cards (for mother) had its poem printed in imitation handwriting, so if Mom were in her second childhood, she might be duped into believing that the sentiment was not a hand-me-down, but custom-made, a lyrical outpouring from the sender's overflowing heart.

> "Mother dear, you're wonderful!
> In everything you do!
> The happiness of fam'ly life
> Depends so much on you.

Or more subtly,

> You put the sweet in home sweet home
> By the loving things you do.
> You make the days much happier
> By being so sweet too.

"The mother of the greeting card inhabits a delicious Disneyland, where everything is syrup and technicolor, cuteness and schmaltz. And this, I reflected . . . is all that remains of the cult of the Great Mother, the oldest and, in many ways, the profoundest of all religions.

"For Paleolithic Man, every day was Mother's Day. Far more sincerely than a modern purchaser of greeting cards, he believed that 'Mother dear, you're wonderful.' Just how wonderful is attested by the carvings of Mother unearthed in the caves which, 20,000 years ago, served our ancestors as cathedrals . . . Mother was felt to be analogous to the fruitful earth and, for centuries, her images were apt to exhibit all the massiveness of her cosmic counterparts.

"How is it that we have permitted ourselves to become so unrealistic, so flippantly superficial in our everyday thinking and feeling about man and the world he lives in?

"'The happiness of family life depends so much on you.' This apparently is as deep as the popular mind is prepared to go into the subject of mother. And the minority opinion of those who have graduated from greeting cards to Dr. Freud is hardly more adequate. For our ancestors, as we have seen, mother was not only the particular person who made or marred the happiness of family life, she was also the visible embodiment of a cosmic mystery . . . Mother was the source of physical life, the principle of fecundity. But the principle of fecundity is also, in the very nature of things, the principle of mortality; for the giver of physical life is also, of necessity, the giver of death . . . wherever she has been worshipped—and there is no part of the world in which, at one time or another, she has not been worshipped—the Great Mother is simultaneousely the creator and the destroyer . . . To cope with the mysteries of experience modern man has no such cosmic symbol as the Great Mother . . . Will it ever be possible to revive the Great Mother, or create some equivalent symbol of the cosmic mysteries of life and death? Or are we doomed indefinitely . . . on the level of the greeting card. Triviality and make-believe are much more easily turned to economic advantage that realistic profundity. . ."

Characteristically, in sending my non-Mother's Day greeting to my favorite nonmother, I have done almost exactly what Mr. Huxley so justly criticizes. I have used somebody else's words. Perhaps you and the ghost of Mr. Huxley will forgive me because of their excellence and because, like calligraphers of old, I did write them out in my own hand, and they carry with grace my deepest love.

T he day Gandhi was assassinated twenty years ago, the French writer, Andre Gide, wrote in his journal: "Gandhi has just been murdered by a Hindu . . . two days ago already a bomb had been thrown at him. It was too beautiful, it was unbelievable, that mystical victory in which spiritual ardour held brutality at a respectful distance; my heart is filled with admiration for that superhuman figure; filled with sobs. This is like a defeat for God, a step backwards."

Events have often made me feel that which Gide so movingly expressed: "that it has been like a defeat for God, a step backwards." I will spare you, my love, a calender of public tragedies and personal sorrows. But the other day when the Supreme Court of the United States (one of the frailest that ever has sat together, one of the most potentially repressive) announced that the death penalty procedures in Ohio and California did not violate the Constitution, that a jury did have the right and power to decide between life and death; Gide's powerful, poignant and beautiful phrase occurred to me instantly.

I am too literary by far; it is not that I have read too much (an impossibility) but that I have retained it all like some besotted, indiscriminate pedagogue and not put it to brilliant use like a Julian or Aldous Huxley. And, alas, I am perfectly serious, although I am not putting myself in the same glorious class with the Huxley brothers (and their grandfather, for that matter): let me be a grim object lesson to you. On my deathbed I will doubtless come up with the perfect phrase: someone else's. Few there are who think their own thoughts and feel their own feelings. It was Albert Einstein who wrote that. You see, it's hopeless, or more to the point, I am hopeless, but as the Austrians would say, not serious.

I could always plagiarize, of course; and to compound my particular brand of addiction I could, at least, justify plagiarism by telling you that T.S. Eliot says a good poet does not borrow, he steals. And sweepingly, majestically, Eliot followed his own dictum. But I am saved from this temptation because I am not a poet at all, and besides, deliberate deception makes losers of us all, especially of the deceiver whose cleverness wears away truth until he has no discernment left. It is not that honesty is the best policy, it is that truth and love are the sole instruments for sanity, humanity and survival. Have I said that before? It cannot be repeated too often.

Once when I was walking down the main street of Palo Alto, one of our famous local psychologists hailed me in his big cheerful voice. Even with his severely stooped posture, he stood a sturdy, vigorous figure of six feet four.

"Do you have a moment, Ira? I have a problem."

His booming voice was serious and mocking, as was habitual with him. We were old friends.

"I do" I said, "What is your problem, doctor?"

Over cups of coffee he told me of a thirty-eight-year old man who had lived an apparently happy conventional life with a wife and two children until one morning on his way to work he stopped, raped a 2-1/2 year old child, murdered her, threw her into some bushes, and without troubling much to conceal his deed, started to walk toward the bus station. The police caught him in a matter of hours.

When my friend first saw him, this man was in the locked examining room of a prison mental hospital. He was gibbering incomprehensibly. But with individual and group therapy he not only recovered rapidly, he also developed a real skill in helping other inmates. Now cured, the state could, and was about to execute him. By law, you understand, one has to be in sound physical and psychological health in order to enjoy one's execution to the full.

The man was sent to "death row" at San Quentin. He was waiting to be taken to the gas chamber, once again gibbering incomprehensibly.

My friend G. showed me some of the letters he had received from the prisoner. They were deranged and incoherent, interspersed with bizarre religious allusions. Only one thing was clear. He was begging G. to visit him.

"Well," I said, "you have to go see him, that's all."

"Ira", he said, "I have one ligitimate reason not to go. I have come not to like him. When he was getting better, I found his arrogance insupportable and took myself off the case. Because if you don't like someone you can be of no help

94

whatever."

"Then, G." I said, "You have to write him a letter and tell him why you're not coming."

He leaned back his massive, cerebral head and roared his Titan's laughter, saying: "By God, Ira, we are stuck with truth and love, aren't we?"

I hope this long digression brings us neatly back to the death penalty and the United States Supreme Court. Their decision could unleash the carrying out of an immense number of death sentences in California alone, although the California State attorney general said that he did not "anticipate a wave of executions." He went on to assure us that *only twenty four* of the 99 persons under death sentences in California had their sentences affirmed. Only twenty four! Only one! What fantastic, fathomless arrogance; deliberately to take the life of one person. It is equivalent to saying that God or Nature or what you will, has made a mistake and you, in your greater wisdom, will correct it!

Bernard Shaw said it with distinct, vivid, pragmatic wit: "Criminals do not die by the hands of the law. They die by the hands of other men. Assassination on the scaffold is the worst form of assassination, because there it is invested with the approval of society . . . murder and capital punishment are not opposites that cancel one another, but similars that breed their kind." (See Arthur Koestler's *Reflections on Hanging,* New York, 1957; James Avery Joyce's *Capital Punishment,* New York, 1961; Curtis Bok's *Star Wormwood,* New York, 1959; Karl Menninger's *The Crime of Punishment,* New York, 1969)

The facts of history corroborate Shaw. Only the sentimentalists hold to the preservation of the death penalty.

In the Western democracies, every country has abolished capital punishment except France and the United States. Although there are, I believe, ten American states that have abolished it completely and four others that only invoke it for so called 'exceptional crimes': treason, piracy and the killing of a policeman.

Later this year, because of another case, the United States Supreme Court could redeem itself and all of us by deciding that the death penalty is unconstitutional because it is cruel and unjust punishment. What could be crueler? more unjust? to know the exact time, date and place of your most involuntary unnatural death? I shudder.

On the other hand, the Supreme Court could decide that the death penalty was not cruel and unjust, or it could merely evade the question legalistically. If that happens, it will be like a defeat for God, a step backwards.

On May 6th, *The New York Review of Books* published a translation of an open letter to Fidel Castro that first appeared April 9th, in the French newspaper *Le Monde*.

The open letter deals with Herberto Padilla, one of Cuba's finest poets. Earlier he had received Cuba's highest poetry award in spite of the Cuban army and the communist party's attempt to have it denied him—the latter are just not very fond of people thinking for themselves, especially when they express themselves publicly and clearly.

In Havana on March 20th, Senor Padilla was arrested and imprisoned without charges or trial; something Castro promised would never happen in the Cuba of his regime.

The open letter to Castro was written to express "disquiet as a result of the imprisonment of the poet and writer, Herberto Padilla, and to ask you to reexamine the situation which the arrest has created. Since the Cuban government up to the present time has yet to supply any information about the arrest, we fear the reemergence of a sectarian tendency stronger and more dangerous than that which you denounced in 1962, and to which Major Che Guevara alluded on several occasions when he denounced the suppression of the right of criticism within the ranks of the revolution."

A long and impressive list of European and Latin American intellectuals who are "supporters of the principles and objectives of the Cuban Revolution" signed the letter.

I am glad the letter was written. It is good, compelling, generous. But the answer has already come: gloomy, ghastly, familiar. Stalin now wears a Cuban face. *Le Monde* reported that Castro himself "had personally ordered the arrest of Padilla." And he denounced the "bourgeois intellectuals" who had written the open letter, although he did not tell his audience at the First National Congress of Education and Culture that the names of the signatories included Jean-Paul Sartre, Simone De Beauvior, and four of the greatest Latin American novelists: Julio Cortazor, Gabriel Garcia Marquez, Carlos Fuentes, and Maria Vargas Llosa.

Le Monde also reported that Padilla was released on

April 27th, and that he read a statement of self-criticism written in jail saying that he was an Iago (Othello's treacherous betrayer) a counter-revolutionary, and so on.

"The language and tone of his self-denounciation" says *Le Monde* "are so unlike that of his work and his personal manner that an old friend, the Cuban novelist Juan Atchocha declared that 'it could have only been extracted under torture.'"

And all of this was engineered by the man who in 1953 said that the opponents of the Batista regime suffered "barbaric tortures practiced upon them by the repressive security forces." And furthermore he added that "Cuba should be the bulwark of liberty and not a shameful link in the chain of despotism." (See Fidel Castro—*History Will Absolve Me*, London, 1968)

Fidel Castro said these things eighteen years ago in a Cuban courtroom before he was sentenced for trying to overthrow the dictator Batista. Was he lying? Of course not. Then what had changed in the interval? Lord Acton explained it clearly in a letter to Bishop Mandell Creighton in 1887: "Power tends to corrupt" Lord Acton wrote the Bishop, "Absolute power corrupts absolutely."

And the poet Shelly drove the point home:

"Power, like a desolating pestilence,
pollutes what'ere it touches."

No social thinker from Confucius to Karl Marx has said anything more important. And it was this that Gandhi, of all politicians, so clearly understood.

Power must be replaced by *satyagraha,* soul force, truth force, or the human race will not survive the corruption inevitably produced by power.

The question is, will we learn this soon enough? The assumption must be yes, even if the facts turns out to be no.

Writing to you yesterday of the Cuban poet Herberto Padilla reminded me of a similar event years before.

In 1957, the editor of the daily newspaper *Algiers Republican* Henri Alleg, was arrested and tortured by French paratroopers (it's reassuring, isn't it, that ferocity is so democratically shared). Alleg was held and tortured daily for one month. In spite of the torture he wrote the book *The Question*, describing it almost as it was happening and had the book smuggled out of prison. (See the hardbound edition of Alleg's *The Question*, New York, 1958. The introduction Sartre wrote for it is one of his finest essays.)

The book was not in the French bookstores very long before it was seized by the French government and banned (Not DeGaulle, but the socialist Mollet headed the republic at that time). One month later, due to the tireless work of a number of people and, most importantly, to an open "solemn petition to the President of the Republic," signed by eminent French writers of all political and religious persuasions, Alleg was taken out of the hands of the French army, and his book once again made available to the public. Sartre's name appears both on the open letter to Fidel Castro and on the petition to the President of the Republic. Had Sartre been born in England or the United States instead of France, his existentialism would have led him to Gandhi instead of Marx.

More recently, the young French Marxist writer, Regie Debray, a co-worker of Che Guevara was, by similar petitionings, released from a Bolivian prison while serving a thirty-year sentence. All of this is to the good. I'm glad all these men were released (though Alleg and Padilla may be tragically broken).

Every man and woman should be released from prison.

In a broad sense all prisoners are political prisoners. Besides, jails and prisons do nothing but brutalize the inmates, broaden their criminal techniques, and make certain that crime is increased.

As an old jail bird I can attest that the jails themselves are one of the worst crimes. And even if no intelligent, humane, and temporary restraining institutions were put in their place, which could be easily done, but even if they were not and all the jails and prisons were abolished, which they should be, I can assure you that the streets of the world, certainly the streets of America, would be safer.

And as you can imagine, numbered for the inside and nameless to the outside, most men and women sit listlessly in prison with no voice raised for them, no letter from the prominent, no petition from the distinguished.

I am by no means begrudging the writers their almost divine pardon. I just wish the almost divine pardon were universal.

In three perfect stanzas of W. H. Auden's poem "In Memory of W. B. Yeats" Auden records the writer's unparalleled good fortune:

> Time that is intolerant
> Of the brave and innocent,
> And indifferent in a week
> To a beautiful physique,
>
> Worships language and forgives
> Everyone by whom it lives.
> Pardons cowardice, conceit,
> Lays its honours at their feet.
>
> Time that with this strange excuse
> Pardoned Kipling and his views,
> And will pardon Paul Claudel,
> Pardon him for writing well.

Barring something phenomenally good or atrociously bad, this should be my last letter on the Indochina war, unless at any time I would hear the marvelous news that the war was over (the phenomenally good) or that nuclear weapons were being used (the atrociously bad).

Reluctantly I turn now to the My Lai massacre. When I first read the story of it, it seemed a horror heaped upon an already indescribable pyramid of horrors. A new-old version of unbelievable barbarity. Yet the details that I read in Seymour Hersh's book, *My Lai 4*, shocked and sickened me more than I would have anticipated. And I have what seems to me a disquieting admission to make. It is this: although the war, which is just an asceptic word to express one long, drawn out massacre and atrocity, continues to shock me, and although I am daily distressed by most of the events I read in the newspapers; nothing, absolutely nothing surprises me now! There seems to be no insane, criminal inhumanity of which we are not capable.

And yet the public response to Lieutenant Calley's part in the massacre has given me pause, a sense of uneasiness and a sense of hope. Many people were confused, not only as to what they should think, but actually as to what they were feeling. It showed that we were once again aware of how monstrous men can be made by the progressive brutalization of war. We saw also something far worse and at the same time something fragilely hopeful.

On the one hand, the whole affair revealed that monstrousness is still acceptable when deemed a military necessity. Conversely, it laid bare, for the first time, that the monster is that very thing called "military necessity."

No recriminations, please. No angry claims that I have subtly manipulated you by mail, that I knew the judicious mixture of charm, humour and self-effacement to "pry you loose from Thomas." Really, as little as we know about ourselves, you know I would not do that, and more importantly, you know that you're nobody's pawn save perhaps your own fears'.

Once when the two Russian writers, Tolstoy and Gorky, were together, Gorky told Tolstoy of a dream he had of a pair of empty, grey felt-topped boots marching slowly over a barely distinguishable road. Tolstoy asked Gorky: "How do you come to have such dreams?"

"I don't know" Gorky said.

"We know nothing about ourselves" Tolstoy said. Then the wise, old Tolstoy sighed and, after a pause, added:

"We know nothing."

Love, I know you know I related the exchange between Gorky and Tolstoy to emphasize that if I were in any way a factor in "prying you loose from Thomas," it was absolutely without deliberate or conscious knowledge. Besides, my guess is that your separation is right and only temporary, and that you will be together again with a greater amount of that most difficult and most necessary ingredient: forbearance. Without it we are almost an unbearable burden to ourselves and to everyone else.

I think this hideous IndoChinese war and the stupid, hurried way in which we live our lives have made us all harder, tougher.

Not only on Thomas, but on yourself, be more merciful. The 19th century English poet priest Gerard Manley Hopkins said it beautifully:

My own heart let me more have pity on; let
Me live to my sad self hereafter kind,
Charitable; not live this tormented mind
With this tormented mind tormenting yet . . .

Soul, self; come, poor jackself, I do advise
You, jaded, let be; call off thoughts awhile

Elsewhere; leave comfort root-room; let joy size
At God knows when to God knows what; whose smile
's not wrung, see you; unforeseen times rather
    -as skies
Between pie mountains—lights a lovely mile.

And because of the not-unwelcome vogue of ecology, let me tell you that Hopkins was an early conservationist, a premature ecologist; he pleaded:

What would the world be, once bereft
Of wet and of wildness? Let them be left,
O let them be left, wildness and wet
Long live the weeds and the wilderness yet.

P.S. A still earlier ecologist was the Buddha who knew that we had to treat nature with the same consideration that we treat man, or we will not survive.
P.P.S. And, you get to be angry with me. Anyone who gives advice deserves it. Moreover, it is the best thing to do with anger: throw it to our friends and the winds, be rid of it and forget it.

What I spared you in P.P.S. yesterday, I'm going to impart today. It may well be the most important of all subjects with which to attempt to achieve social liberation. (A modest manner in which to begin a letter.)

It was Tolstoy who suggested it:

"If a man has learned to think" he wrote, "he is always thinking of his own death."

Tolstoy did not say 'thinking fearfully of his own death,' but I would, for fearful it is, for most of us, most of the time. And this, it seems to me, is substantiated by the grim and correct observation of the famous American jurist, Oliver Wendell Holmes, Jr. Bluntly (and God knows, maybe with approval; I hope not, I do not know) he said: "Every society rests on the death of men."

Death, then, is at the root of all of our fears: personal and social, mental, biological and physical. And fears dominate our lives. For example, if each day we kept a balance sheet of all the things we did out of joy, out of a sense of well-being, or love, and of all the things we did or did not do because of fears, large, small, habitual or unexpected, the balance sheet, I would guess, would not be very cheering.

So it is fear that makes us an easy mark for manipulation. It is the stock-in-trade not only of the propagandist of state and industry, the executive and the general, the judge and the prosecutor, the teacher and the student, the preacher and parishoner, the boss and the worker, the police and the thief, the official and the citizen; it is not only the stock in trade of these but also of the boys and girls down the street, brothers and sisters, fathers and mothers, aunts and uncles, friends and lovers; in short, it is all of us, of all ages, of both sexes.

And fear is the prison house in which most of us live, and though we are not invariably the architect, we are often the contractor and always the laborer, hiring our own guards or, even more frequently, standing guard over ourselves. And if we do not succeed in changing this we are doomed at best to remain stunted, cowering, murderous spiritual dwarves; and we will go on perfecting our prison house, calling it a palace of freedom. Or we will indeed have a war that will end all wars because we will succeed in the ending of life.

Fear, at once spontaneous and assiduously inculcated, is the enemy, and death is its master.

But, it's of absolutely no help to tell people who are afraid of not being popular, of not doing well at school, of not advancing in their careers, of not being adequate lovers, or who are afraid of communists, capialists, blacks, whites, Jews, Arabs, Mexicans, Orientals, foreigners, or of whomever or of whatever, it is no help to tell these people that their fear is the fear of death. We must deal with the fears in the forms in which they appear. And if we are able to deal with them specifically (and not superficially) but without solemnity, we shall put them to rest, and at the same time, sometimes consciously, sometimes not, we shall have passed through the fear of death.

It is a protective, tragically deluded state of mind. It is why the wisdom of the child is in his do-it-now impatience, and the wisdom of the adult in the delicate balance of action and patience.

Once we discover and face our mortality we discover the preciousness of life, we discover love, the priceless gift we exchange with one another. Then death is dead and love is abroad in the land. Hurray and damn, because it so damnably difficult.

P.S. Read Tolstoy's *The Death of Ivan Ilytch.* It is not a story but an illumination.

*Mid to
Late May
1971*

I t is eventide; an archaic and gently affected word of which I am fond, and a time of day I generally do not write. At this hour, in chosen solitude, I frequently give myself over to melancholy and meditation.

It is in the morning when you vigorously face the world and, with brave words or whatever bravado you prefer, begin to undertake quixotic adventures. But as you and the day wane . . .

"The sun descending in the west,
The evening star does shine;
The birds are silent in their nest
And I must seek for mine."

You come to a perspective, balance and harmony in spite of the murderous outside and the insignificance of your most heroic efforts.

Not only do most people not know that Bach or El Greco ever lived, their great work has not changed in the least the grinding poverty or spiritual squalor of daily life. And does one have to admit the same cheerless fact of the lives of Buddha and Jesus on the lives of billions living now? Yes. To date they have not substantially touched the man in the street, the slum or the village.

Starvation, slavery and sufferings have not been routed. Except for a privileged few, their dominion is thorough and only speciously and pathetically challenged.

And what of the would-be violent saviors? Robespierre, Marx, Lenin, Mao? Although my personal and political bias would like me to answer that they have unequivocally worsened the lot of man, I would have to say the same as I did for the Buddha or Jesus: to date, for the majority of the people, they have effected nothing at all.

With this harsh, sweeping observation there would be much disagreement. And it would be reasonable, which would be its chief error, and it would be passionate, which would be its greatest appeal.

But man is becoming progressively hungrier. Look up the depressing (because not acted upon) and informative writings of the late John Boyd Orr, British nutritionist and agricultural scientist.

Hunger and war perpetuate each other and deepen the impoverishment. And so long as there is war, even the minority of the well-fed; indeed, every man, woman and child on earth, is a prisoner of war condemned to life imprisonment or the death penalty. Who will release them? What Ralph Nader will attack and do away with the institution of war?

Only the prisoners can free themselves, yet it is they who finance and man the industry, carry out the orders and execute themselves. Who would believe it, except for the lemmings?

Such were my meditations as the sun sank and night deepened the kinship of Palo Alto to all other towns in the world.

And no matter what my meditations, I think of you. I thought particularly of your recent interest in living in a commune.

There is certainly a communal movement afoot in this country and Europe, in Asia and in Africa as well. It is without question an important part of what Theodore Roszak first called the counter culture. The New York Times reports that there are over 2000 communes in the United States alone. Their breadth in style, purpose and ethic is huge, which makes them all the more interesting. I know of only three first-hand, having stayed in the Peace Brigade commune in Berkeley, which is friendly, nonviolent and political. The young people impressed me favorably, but they are packed too tightly together for my taste and, surprisingly, for some of theirs. I also stayed in a Franciscan Monastery outside of Naples, Italy. It too was friendly and involved in the local politics. The monks seemed to get on well. I shared none of their theological views and they were unpatronizingly tolerant. I also visited Thomas Merton in a Trappist monastery in Kentucky. It seemed not unlike a British public school (or an American Prep school), and I was not much taken with it, though I liked Merton a great deal.

I know many communes at one remove, having young friends (and some not so young) living in them, and of course I have read about them—from the early ascetic Essene communes to the group marriage ones. For although the communes are the latest up-to-date fashion in living for the radical young, they have a widespread, ancient history. And today, along with the experimental communal living are some that still retain the most traditional religious forms. What underlies all of them is the willingness and the desire to share. The mortality rate, for many reasons, is high. Those that seem and seemed to do the best are the ones that combine to a high degree explicit common aspirations, good will, tact, discipline, intelligence and space. The last is of the utmost importance, and I mean space both in the physical and psychological sense.

For all ages there seem to be some advantages living in such a manner, provided that the sharing is, for the most part responsible, joyful and spontaneous. When this arrangement goes well, understanding and appreciation are developed and practiced.

Theoretically, at any rate, there is greater flexibility for each person within the commune than within the small family. The greater flexibility comes from the wider and deeper participation, without which you have created another prison—one of chaos or regimentation. What constitutes privacy as opposed to aloofness varies, and has to be sensitively worked out.

Sex, "the lion of the tribe of human passions," often, though not invariably undermines many of these experiments, but probably no more than it does outside communal living.

My deepest apprehension, from what I've seen and from what I have read, is the swiftness with which the communards became exclusive, tribal and conformist. And all too often these characteristics, albeit unconsciously, are assumed as virtues.

I am all in favor of the experiments. They may turn out to be historically important, although they may be of a brief duration. But when we forget that we are experimenters in a changing world, rigidity sets in.

We achieve a modicum of stability when we learn how to make intelligent loving change; which means that tradition should not be thoughtlessly kept or discarded. We should select from the past what sustains us and not what strangles

111

us, and know that the new is not intrinsically harmful or helpful to life simply because it is new. We have to be eclectic.

Until recently, the word commune was associated principally with the Paris Commune of 1870: "On the dawn of the 18th of March Paris arose to the thunderburst of 'Viva La Commune!' " It was an uprising against the French centralized state power.

Hopefully these communes that are flourishing now are not escapist but a part of an authentic nonviolent alternative—a counter culture—to the centralized state powers.

Perhaps the thunderburst, of all things, will have brought forth fresh flower children. Bouquets instead of barricades. A new world from a petal of a flower, not from a barrel of a gun.

Two days of flu and fever, thus two days of being incapable of writing any letters. The fever, as fever will, not only weakened me, but seemed to remove me to some unknown place. I was here and I was not. It was not wholly agreeable nor disagreeable. I listened to Mozart, I began reading Julian Huxley's autobiography, *Memories*.

"I was born with great advantages—genetic and cultural," he writes in the preface, "but there were disadvantages, too." I am not a little envious of those genes and culture; it was rather an extraordinary combination which will certainly not happen again.

Anyway, I am fine today and I want to return to you and my remembrance of Martin Luther King.

The last time I saw Martin was in 1968. He and his colleague, Rev. Andrew Young, were visiting me in Santa Rita, a county jail in Oakland, California. I was serving a 90-day sentence, 45 days suspended, for deliberately standing in the way of a busload of army inductees. The official charge was disturbing the peace. I recall that the young inductees, on that December morning, looked downcast, whereas the protestors were chattering and cheerful, having happily and voluntarily accepted the determined and courteous discipline of satyagraha.

In jail, I was being held in maximum security. (You cannot be too careful with these vicious men who refuse to kill, for they may spread their dangerous and criminal ideas to other inmates, which would interfere with the jail's splendid program of rehabilitation which the men like so much that it keeps them returning to it again and again.) I wrote postcards to friends during that time, ironically beginning: "In case you did not know it, I am wintering in Santa Rita."

"Thank you for coming to see me," I said to Martin and Andy. (I had known Andy as long as I had known Martin, which was a little over three years). I was struck, in my solid middle class fashion, by how clean they looked, how fresh their white shirts appeared. I stared at them, especially at their clothes, with amused and tender envy. I had not been

113

able to change my prison garb of blue jeans and a shirt of thin blue cotton for almost thirty days.

"Well, Martin, how are the plans progressing for the Poor People's March?" I asked.

"They are not clear yet," he said, "but they will be."

"Don't go to Washington," I urged, "Decentralize and have the demonstration or demonstrations in every part of the country exactly where the poor are living."

"It is only the federal government that has the needed money and power," Martin said.

"That's because we have allowed it to have both."

"The people want to go to Washington," he insisted.

We had had that kind of argument before, and I had always lost, or more precisely, I think we both had lost. Turning to Andy, but still watching Martin, I asked: "What in general do you think is going to happen?"

Gloomily, Martin answered: "You know that Dr. Spock has been indicted for the so-called conspiracy of aiding and abetting young men not to join the armed forces. And there are pretty well-founded rumours that there are roughly forty more indictments ready to be handed out."

"You won't get one," I predicted, "not a black Nobel Peace Prize winner, the government wouldn't dare."

"Not even after the famous baby doctor?" Martin asked.

"Not even after the famous baby doctor," I repeated.

"Things are going to get worse" Andy hazarded. "The Poor People's March will be some kind of turning point."

"Unfortunately I agree that things are going to get worse," I said, "but I don't think that the Poor People's March will affect anything unless it is decentralized and sustained over a long period of time. Only if people understand and act upon *satyagraha* will we get out of this century alive. Toynbee's right, Gandhi will be the prophet of the 20th century, if there is a 21st."

As I spoke, I noticed for the first time how uneasy both Martin and Andy seemed. Martin frequently looked down at his brilliantly shined shoes and Andy's gaze kept wandering along the pale green walls of the visitors' cell. For a multitude of reasons, some of which I could guess and some I could not, Martin and Andy seemed eager to leave. It is like that when you visit friends in jail. You want them to be out, or to be

114

yourself sharing their incarceration.

It could have been a scene from Tolstoy's last novel, *Resurrection*. Tolstoy had never been in prison, but there was not a corner of man's journey that Tolstoy's vision had not penetrated.

I rang for the guard to unlock the door so that Martin and Andy could go, and I, return to my six-by-six cell, which I shared with another prisoner.

As they were leaving, Martin said: "You're a fine courageous man, Ira, and our prayers are with you."

I smiled. "Martin, you know I'm not a bit courageous, but I'm delighted to have your prayers."

He was on his way out, then he stopped, turned around and said: "Ira, I have a favor to ask of you."

"Anything," I said, "I'm a captive audience."

"When I'm in jail in Washington," he said, "come visit me there."

"It's a promise," I said. And it was a promise I would like to have kept, perhaps more than any. But as you and the whole world know, Martin did not get to Washington. In April of that year he was shot to death in Memphis, Tennessee.

At the time, Joan Baez, David Harris and I were at Cornell University on a country-wide speaking tour, which I shall write you about later.

Ira

P.S. I am glad you and Thomas are drawing closer again and may, once more, be living together. I wish I could write that I feel not the slightest trace of envy. I could, but it would be a lie.

This will be short letter to answer your questions and principally, as always, to carry my love.

As I have previously written, I will welcome a call from Thomas about his heroin and draft difficulties. In general, I know a great deal about the latter and very little of the former, although not long ago a young actor friend of mine died of an overdose of heroin. Which increased my apprehension decidedly more than my knowledge.

On this subject Thomas should, if he hasn't already, get good, sympathetic professional help, which does not at all mean that I wouldn't be happy to talk with him. By the way, I am fairly certain that my telephone is tapped from time to time, because I am (quote) "a well-known California Pacifist." (I suppose I'm well known to other California pacifists.) So if Thomas calls, he may not only be talking to me, but also to whomever is assigned to listen to California Pacifists. It doesn't bother me in the least; there is nothing I say that anyone is not welcome to hear, but I do not like the police state portent of it. Besides, the poor professional eavesdropper must get bored with my conversations. Anyway, I thought Thomas should know.

Once when I was in a hotel in New York City with my friend Andy Young. We knew that our rooms were "bugged." I asked Andy what he did under the circumstances.

"Ira," he said, "I just preach to them." Naturally that appealed to me. So do you. The King-Spock-Baez-Harris-/Sandperl story continues tomorrow.

After Martin's and Andy Young's visit in jail; after the knowledge of the indictment of Dr. Spock, and the rumor that there were fory more indictments to be handed out, depending (I speculated) on the outcome of the Spock trial, I concentrated my thoughts on the variety of nonviolent actions we could take.

You have plenty of time for such or any other meditations in maximum security, once you accustom yourself to the incessant high level of noise. Men carry on conversations by literally yelling at one another unless they are content to talk with their friends in the cells near them, which most are not. I scarcely spoke at all unless I was asked questions by other inmates, which happened frequently. My grey hair made me some sort of respected arbiter.

The rumors that Martin repeated were, in the main, reliable. So what I decided was that after my release from jail, Joan, David and I should go on a country wide speaking tour, recreating as often as possible, with as many people as possible, the act that had brought about Dr. Spock's indictment. His conspiracy charges included the signing of a statement urging all draft age young men to refuse to go into the armed services, a "call to resist illegitimate authority" and his publicly asking for and accepting the draft cards that all young men are, by law, required to carry with them all the time. It was complicity in non-cooperating with the Selective Service Act.

Not only would Joan, David and I deliberately commit Dr. Spock's "crime," but we would also urge, in as many ways as we could think of, nonviolent resistance to the war in Vietnam with emphasis on civil disobedience and a refusal to pay that portion of our income tax that is alloted to the military.

My guess was that the government thought it could silence the whole anti-war movement if it could silence Dr. Spock. The government, in my opinion, had made, for its own purposes, an immense blunder and had selected absolutely the wrong man. Dr. Spock is not a radical of any kind. He is a Yankee of Yankees, an elderly, alert, elegant, silverhaired, New England partician. Added to this, he is no snob, but personable, kind and humorous.

Joan and David enthusiastically agreed on our making a speaking tour together. David had made many similar tours by himself as the founder of The Resistance (to military conscription), and Joan and I had been on tours both together and separately, but this was the first time the three of us would be travelling together. The moment seemed right, although timing can only be judged in retrospect.

David would soon be going to prison for refusing induction into the army, so many young men were eager to hear him, wondering agonizingly if they could do what he could.

Joan is a magician. She can commune instantly and profoundly with one person or with a thousand—of any age, of either sex. She can do a St. Francis with animals as well. A good concert of hers, and most of them are good, is in the class of a Bach Brandenberg, of *Hamlet*, of *War and Peace*. And others, young and old, wanted ideas and inspiration as to how they could be of help in trying to stop the war and all the varieties of social repression.

In a sense, I would be on the tour as a representative, more or less, of the Spock generation, to say what we, over thirty, could do to help build that world community that men and women have always dreamed of. More concretely, I wanted to assist in making sure that the Spock indictment boomeranged, politically, socially and psychologically. And of course, whenever I speak in public or in private, I try to express something of the importance and moving beauty of Gandhi's *satyagraha* and its manifold applications for America and the world.

At the outset of the tour, David Harris was paged through the loudspeaker system of the airport. Joan and I sat down in glum silence, not concealing our misery as we watched David disappear down an escalator. The federal authorities, we felt, had struck much sooner than we had anticipated.

In unhesitating and full accord, Joan and I agreed to go on with the tour in spite of this unexpected turn.

Joan's intelligent, able young secretary, Carol Solomon, asked if she could get us anything.

"Yes" Joan said, "David." And in a twinkling, Carol succeeded; David was back, smiling his tender boyish smile. David Harris, was also the name of the manager of the airport.

The tour began.

It was late March. And for the most part it was a happy tour, personally and politically. Joan and David got married. The response we received in most places was generous and encouraging. Dr. Spock, found guilty, was acquitted on an appeal.

But late in the night of April 4th, when we were at Cornell University in Ithaca, New York, Carol Solomon knocked at the door of my motel room. She said: "I just heard that Martin Luther King was shot."

"Is he alive or dead?" I asked.

"I don't know" she said. "The night clerk who told me didn't know either. Shall I wake Joan and David and tell them?"

"We'll tell them tomorrow when we know more about it."

"I'm sorry to have disturbed you, Ira, but I saw your light on and thought you would want to know."

"You are absolutely right. Thank you, Carol."

When she had gone, I tried to reach everyone I knew in Memphis, Tennessee, for I knew Martin had gone there to take part in the garbage collectors' strike. But all the lines to Memphis were busy. Then I called my friends in Atlanta, Georgia, but everyone I knew was in Memphis. Then I telephoned the New York Times. And like most people who do not believe in a personal God and do not pray, I was praying that Martin was alive.

The operator at the Times, when I asked her about Martin, said: "Just a moment please, I'll switch you to the King tape."

On tape so fast, I thought. Soon they will have events on tape before they take place. Maybe they already do. And all the time I was praying: "That man who believed in you, let him be alive."

The voice on the tape told me where in Memphis Martin was shot, what ambulance transported him, what hospital received him and the precise time he died. The tape ended by thanking me for my inquiry. And with a mechanical fatuity surpassing that of the tapes, I said "Thank you."

At five a.m. I talked to Andy Young. In a sad, composed voice he said: "Everybody's doing all right considering the awful thing that has happened."

He asked me if Joan and I were coming to the funeral. I told Andy I couldn't answer for Joan, but I would have her call him as soon as she woke up. But as for myself, the answer was no. If it were for Martin's family, for himself and the staff, the answer would be yes. But he knew, I knew, it was going to be a political mockery, a T.V. extravaganza in which I didn't want any part. Andy did not argue.

After I hung up I cried more than I can ever remember crying. Then I went to bed, and to complete the night of infantile insanity,I cursed the God I did not believe in.

P.S. Joan did not go to the funeral.
P.P.S. I have yet to tell you how and where Martin and I first met. Tomorrow's letter begins that episode.

A session of the Institute for the Study of Nonviolence was just over. Those were the days when only Joan and I conducted the seminars. (Now there is an intelligent, young, engaging staff of 20).

Joan was in San Francisco visiting her younger sister Mimi. Mimi has a good voice, plays the guitar well, and is, without question, the most spectacularly beautiful young woman I have ever seen. I hope she meets a Rembrandt who does her portrait.

Mimi's luck has been as bad as she is beautiful, beginning with being a member of an international celebrity's family. "Are you Joan Baez's sister?" It is incessant and endless and Mimi hears it *ad nauseum.* Moreover, her charming, charged with life young writer-husband was killed in a motorcycle accident.

It is my impression that her fortunes have now taken a new and happier turn. Yet whenever I see her, her bewitching and fathomlessly sad blue eyes appear to be on the edge of flooding the earth with tears.

Anyway, Mimi and Joan were in San Francisco at Mimi's small attractive house. They like being together. They laugh a great deal, about themselves, and about their family.

At the same time I was at Stanford University some 30 miles away.

In the morning newspaper, the San Francisco Chronicle, I read that nine black children were savagely beaten in a place called Granada, Mississippi. They were walking to the town's first integrated school when they were struck down by lead pipes in the hands of grown white men. The men were not so-called hoodlums, but members of the respectable middle class. In an instant I decided to join the children.

I telephoned Joan and told her the story. Before I could say or even intimate that I was going to Mississippi, she said: "When do we leave for Granada, Ira?"

God, it was no wonder that I had loved her since the day I had met her, when she was sixteen years old. At sixteen she would have said the same thing. At six hundred she will still be saying the same thing. It is not that Joan is fearless, she

121

has her fears, but her courage and composure are extra-ordinary. And like Jacob, she also has her angel with whom she wrestles. And like Jacob, one dawn, after a long, ex-hausting sleepless night, she will arise undefeated.

"We'll go to Granada" I told her, "as soon as I find out how we get there, and if there are any SNCC people (Student Nonviolent Coordinating Committee, or SCLC (Southern Christian Leadership Conference) people already there. Then I'll get our tickets, buy a razor, shave off my beard, and call you back to tell you the time and place to meet me at the San Francisco airport. I'm sure all this can be done very quickly."

"Ira," Joan exclaimed, "I've never seen you without a beard. How will I recognize you? And why are you shaving it?"

"Darling, you'll recognize me easily enough" I assured her, and I will grow a beard back as soon as we return, but I want in Mississippi to look like the nice average middle-class man that I am."

"You won't fool anyone," she teased. "They'll spot that non-killer look in your eye in a moment and you'll be done for."

"I'll keep my eyes demurely lowered."

"You're hopeless," she said.

"Of course. But in spite of everything we both have hope and you know it!"

"We're crazy." She laughed and hung up.

That afternoon at the San Francisco airport, after every-thing had been easily arranged by Martin Luther King's SCLC office in Atlanta, Georgia, Joan and I met as planned. When she saw me she said: "My God, you look like a survivor from Dachau who has not made up his mind whether he is glad he's survived or not." Curiously I had thought precisely that when I first saw my naked face in the mirror.

Two SCLC field secretaries picked us up at the Memphis airport and drove us to Granada. I sat in front with the older of the two men, and Joan was in back with the younger. They were both friendly and helpful. Joan and the young man were immediately laughing and talking easily. My companion was perfectly nice, but though he was alledgedly addressing his remarks to me, they were meant for Joan and they were

122

meant to impress her, which was understandable but a little tiresome.

I asked when they were expecting Dr. King.

"The following day," I was told.

"But if you want to get something across to him," the younger field secretary said, "you have to get to Andy Young first. Dr. King doesn't   ," he hesitated several seconds, then blurted out: "Dr. King doesn't piss without first asking Andy."

"Now, now," the older man said reprovingly.

"You know it's true" the young man persisted.

And suddenly all four of us not very taciturn people were silent. Then, after two or three miles, the older man swelled and blew out his cheeks in a concentrated stream of laughter that rattled the windows.

"Robert is really right" he said, "Dr. King doesn't piss without asking Andy's okay."

We drove to the one black church in Granada and were introduced to the SCLC staff and to the volunteers. There was one white among them, a young man on loan from SNCC.

Everyone was unaffectedly cordial except one very handsome, very black young man who was a regular staff member. He loathed us instantaneously. To give him his due, I do not think it was a hasty superficial judgment. I am certain he detested us long before he met us. He was unhappy about the house that had been selected for us. My feeling was that he wanted our white noses to be rubbed into the worst shanty in Granada. And Joan and I further infuriated him by saying we wanted to be put where we could cause everyone the least inconvenience. Robert, the young field secretary, insisted the house assigned to us was done with that in mind.

It was comfortable two-bedroom frame house, filled with bric-a-brac and goodwill. What I liked best, after the owner, was that almost invariable Southern front porch sheltering two old rocking chairs.

The owner was a sturdy, cheerful, hard-working widow who made us feel at home at once. She was a chamber maid in an all-white motel. When her employer learned that she was active in the civil rights movement, he threatened to fire her. She was not intimidated. She told him she intended to go on working for Dr. King as long as she lived. The employer never mentioned it again. He was no fool; she was a good and thorough worker.

Joan and I left our few things at the house and returned to the church to meet many more people, young and old. The church in Granada, as in countless small towns throughout the South, was the center of the black people's lives, the sole and complete center. It was a real sanctuary. A real church. I loved it.

Maybe the reason your letter came as such a shock was that I was still caught up in the memory of the beauty of that night in Granada with Joan that I wrote you of yesterday.

But my God!, you are either one of the great liberated women of our time, an uncannonized saint, or a devouring little bitch!

Yes, I am angry and jealous, not in the grand Proustian manner but in the smaller Sandperlian way with an aggravating, perceptibly empty, uncomfortable feeling in my stomach. I should have said so when you first took up with Thomas, but I was not going to give you the pleasure nor myself the pain. Or perhaps I was not really jealous then.

But I am now that you have taken this Francis, whose last name you don't seem to know, into your house and bed, and have invited Thomas to live with you as well because he is "so sick and lost."

Do you plan to sleep with them both? Or just drive them both crazy? You can do it all simultaneously while reading them my letters.

And you laughed and agreed with that cretin Francis when he told you that my writing was like late Richardson and early Trollope. Very pretty, very witty, though it is obvious he has read neither. Well, thank him for me. It is a compliment.

Whom does he read, if he can read? Herman Wouk? or has he graduated to Truman Capote?

He says I am a gap of centuries rather than that of a generation. Your humorist is more jealous than I and for a boy of 20 he has an inspiring grasp of cliches. There's nothing I like about him.

Perhaps now I will act out a cliche myself: go to a brothel, reel in the night streets and curse women . . .

P.S. No, I am not going to do any of these things, instead I shall follow the keener example of St. Ignatius Loyola who, when asked what his feelings would be if the Pope were to suppress The Company of Jesus, answered: "A quarter of an hour of prayer, and I should think no more about it."

Moreover, it is not true that there is nothing I like about your new lover. I like his name. It reminds me of Francis of Assisi, the most lovable of Christians, whose prayers, songs and general gaity I admire. And if I or anyone lived out his prayer, even to a tiny degree, there would be no more self pitying, evil tempers. This is how it goes:

"Lord, make me an instrument of Thy peace.
Where there is hatred, let me sow love;
Where there is injury, pardon;
Where there is doubt, faith;
Where there is despair, hope;
Where there is darkness, light;
Where there is sadness, joy.

Oh, Divine Master, grant that I
    may not so much seek to be
    consoled as to console,
To be understood, as to understand
To be loved, as to love.

For it is only in giving that we receive;
It is in pardoning that we are pardoned;
It is in dying that we are born to eternal life."

P.P.S. Deracinate the body of the letter and let the post-scripts remain.

After hours of brooding, I discover I love you more late at night and reluctantly conclude that you and your Francis showed real nobility in inviting Thomas to live with you. It was a stroke of compassion and heroism. You know how demanding it is to be day by day with someone who is seriously trying to get off heroin. But there's no question that it is better for him not to live alone.

You and Francis will have to follow as best you can the Gandhian injunction: "Tender as a lotus and hard as granite," and the Biblical: "Wise as a serpent and harmless as a dove."

Saving bodies and souls in a world that seems to crumble them so easily is a matter of informed skill, love and luck.

And I will await Thomas's phone call tonight about his draft difficulties. You know I think that the best position, politically, socially, psychologically and morally, is complete, open, nonviolent, noncooperation with the Selective Service Act. This is the position of the young men in the Resistance which David Harris began. Even to apply for conscientious objector status in America today is to acknowledge and strengthen the dominion of the state over the lives of these young men. Not only is conscription obsolete and obscene, but so is the whole military apparatus, voluntary or involuntary, governmental or so-called revolutionary.

No young man should have to prove to members of a draft board that he is a conscientious objector to war. They should try to explain to him why they are not. Then they should give a simple apology and dissolve the board. The young man should accept the apology sympathetically and generously, realizing how difficult it is to apologize, and also remembering that they were brought up in a different age, if not pre-historic, certainly pre-atomic.

Paralleling this is that popular and infamous statement by John F. Kennedy: "Do not ask what your country can do for you, but what you can do for your country."

Mr. Kennedy was paying homage to the real victors of World War two: Adolf Hitler, Joseph Stalin, Franklin Roosevelt and Winston Churchill—the men who preferred the nation to man. And all the liberals applauded. They should have wept. Then protested.

When, oh when, will enough of us realize that the ethical is the practical?

To answer my own question: I suppose we will when we are so pushed into the corner that we are forced to see that the only practical way out, no matter how much we hate it, is to cooperate and share equitably, and that no matter how much we love it, we must give up killing one another.

I will do my best not to impose my views on Thomas. And I will help him in every way I can except that I will not help him to dissemble, which is a large part of what we are opposing. Deception would be of no help to him or to that world of decency we long to bring into being.

P.P.P.S. If Thomas is nervous about prison, tell him his many years in school are excellent preparation. I'm only partially joking.

When I went to jail for the first time, I quickly felt at ease because it so reminded me of all my school days. Mind you, I did not like jail any better than I did school (though jail is more honest), but its familiarity was comforting and comical.

My old friend Dave Dellinger once said: "I went from Yale to jail / I learned much more in jail / Than I ever did at Yale."

My conversation with Thomas last night was, if nothing else, long, lively and interesting. I am sorry he feels freer to talk to me when you and Francis are not in the house; doubtless it has to do with the safe distances between our ages and locations, but perfectly selfishly, if you were there, I could at least hear that voice of yours that I love and, at times, miss very much. Tant pis pour moi. Anyway, I'm relieved to hear that Thomas' family is wealthy and that his mother is generous. For if he keeps phoning me, which he says he plans to do, and talks as long as he did, his telephone bill will be huge. Maybe that will diminish his ability to buy so much heroin. On the other hand, I hope it does not deter him from obtaining proper medical or psychiatric help, or whatever one does to get off heroin.

In theory, the answer for him and almost everyone else is easy. There is no heroin, or other drug problem, but a living problem. If your life makes sense to you, if you like yourself, your friends, and what you are doing, then drugs, at the very worst, would be a lark, like your occasional use of grass, an experiment. Certainly not a problem which Americans seem to have an ingenious knack of turning everything into.

Aldous Huxley's two books on psychedelic drugs (never heroin) were, I felt, a major lapse of judgment, taste and responsibility. Genuine modesty, I suppose, must have kept him from telling his readers that his experiments, like those of the New Mexican Indians, were always taken under expert supervision and only after long and disciplined preparation. For example, just one crucial point, Huxley always knew exactly what he was taking and the precise amount of miligrams. His experiments and those of most young men and women had nothing in common except that they both swallowed something: they—God knows what, and he did know.

I do not think that the absence of his books or a more thoughtful presentation of them would have made a marked difference to the so-called drug culture; but they were, alas, an unhelpful and unnecessary imprimatur (imprimatur is the official seal of approval to works endorsed by the Roman

Catholic Church).

It just suits us all too well: illumination in a pill, a sage in a second. I know that's not what Huxley meant, not what he intended. But his wisdom, and he was wise, lost out to the enchanted experimenter and the irrepressible popularizing polymath. It was one time he should have kept his mouth shut or his pen still, or recall his British reserve.

I am told that his friends Thomas Mann and J. Krishnamurti were not only disappointed in him, they were furious. They were right in a way, of course, but the wise are not always wise and, like the rest of us, they have need of compassion, for no matter who, no matter where, no matter what age, no matter what strength, there are times we find ourselves staggeringly lonely.

There is a further paradox in this whole drug use business. The adult middle class population that so stridently condemns the young for their use of drugs, consumes, I would guess, more drugs than the youngsters they condemn. (After all, the world makes no more sense to them than it does to their children.) The only difference is that their drugs are legally prescribed by doctors. Spend some time in a good pharmacy and watch what they decorously dispense in drugs during an average 8 hour period. The pharmacy is the envy of every junkie in the neighborhood.

In my telephone conversation with Thomas last night, he very openly asked what I thought of going underground to avoid the draft, or of going to Canada.

I told him both were humanly and romantically understandable. And I told him over and over again (perhaps too often) that the decision had to be his.

Making a decision, any decision, is his admitted difficulty. If he could, he would make no decision at all. But that, I told him, is an impossibility. Not to make a decision is already a decision not to make a decision. So long as we're alive, we make decisions. It is the same with action. If we tell ourselves we're not going to take any action at this time, that is the action we are taking at this time.

I said that leaving can often have a certain personal appeal. It does not in any way attack the roots of conscription, if he is interested in that; but it does avoid it, if that is what he wants to do . I told him that my maternal

130

great grandfather had come to the United States from Germany to avoid military conscription. Unlike his great-grandson, he was not a pacifist, but felt that conscription of any kind was slavery and would eventually destroy any democratic society in which it was maintained. I dimly recall the stately old flautist. Of course he is dead; and military conscription flourishes.

Going underground, I told Thomas, was damaging because it helped sustain the atmosphere of secrecy, suspicion and distrust in which we already live, and which is one of the paramount factors that make possible the inequalities, the injustices, and the violence we oppose.

And what we must try to do is to show diverse ways of living above the ground. We already live underground in psychological caves.

And, I tried to say these things lightly as well as passionately and with good-humoured humility.

With no more circumlocution, we go back to the South to Joan, and to Martin Luther King.

When Joan and I returned to the church that first evening in Mississippi, we were asked over and over again why we had come to Granada. We were asked good-naturedly and with unrestrained, genuinely welcoming curiosity. We answered that we had read about the children in the newspapers and that we wanted to be of help if we in any way could: with the children, their families, the boycotting of the stores where blacks were automatically not hired, getting the schools integrated . . . whatever.

Actually I thought the schools were so bad, and not just in the South, that the only real value in integrating them was to give the white children (and possibly their parents) a chance to learn something of the lives and culture of their black neighbors, and to free them from the inherited hatred of generations.

Joan sang before we left the church for the night. I have never heard her sing more movingly. One child said to me: "She must have colored blood, don't she? No white person could sing that good."

I laughed: "All our blood is the same."

"You know what I mean," the child persisted.

The next morning we were back in the church early, though a few staff members and I had stayed up late the night before drinking quantities of raw bourbon. Not since those days in Mississippi have I drunk so much and been in church so regularly.

The children assembled at the church each day before leaving for school. Joan and I intended to walk with them. There were newsmen outside, television cameras. They were there because of Joan's presence, because they were expecting Dr. King, and because of the renewed potential of violence.

When we were near the school we were blocked by state troopers; armed, helmeted, and with bellies that dropped down over their cartridge belts. The children were allowed to proceed, but with no one else except their parents.

"We want to see that they get to the school safely," I said

to the troopers in my experienced, pleasantly determined, and unprovocative voice, and the SNCC young man added clearly, courageously and (I felt) gratuitously: "You forget what country you're in."

"There'll be no harm nor difficulty in our walking with the children," I said in a tone I hoped would not further anger the young man or the troopers.

We began to move forward but were again stopped as the troopers drew their lines tighter.

"We have our orders that you are not to go further than this line," one of the troopers volunteered.

"Yeah," almost all of them chorused, which seemed to make them feel less tense, for which I was grateful. The theatrical character of it all, including myself, did not elude me, but I wished the director would have called for a coffee break.

"Who gave you your orders?" I asked.

It was more for the conversation that I spoke than for the information I knew I was not likely to be given. In a situation like this it is important to keep the conversation going, and as naturally as possible. It lessens the isolation, the tension, the fear, the antagonism.

By this time the children had covered the short distance to school and were safely there, though some of them had been turned away.

We went back to the church to plan our afternoon march into town and the picketing of the entire downtown except for the one restaurant where blacks as well as whites were employed and served.

Later in town the white citizenry gathered in little pockets around the square. As I passed a cluster of white men, one whispered to me: "Nigger lover."

"That's progress," I laughingly said. "That's probably the first time in your life you've ever whispered that. Next week you may even be on our picket line."

"I could kill you" he said.

"I don't doubt it," I said, "but living together in some sort of decency, that's the difficult thing we're going to have to learn, that's part of what nonviolence is all about."

Another man staggered out of a store, very drunk. "I got two machine guns, and I'm gonna git ya," he said.

"The funny thing is," said the black young man next to me, "he really does have two machine guns, and he may try to 'git' you."

It was like that every time we were in town; ugly jibes spoken, expecially to Joan, and at least one state trooper patrol car following us everywhere we went. "Security, courtesy, and protection," read the seal on the side of the car. But these were hardly the sentiments they inspired in us.

There were plainclothesmen from the federal justice department, from the FBI, and from the local police. We did not know who was watching whom, or why. Several of the men kept photographing us all the time.

That afternoon Dr. King and Andy Young arrived. And great excitement foliowed their arrival. More newsmen and more and more black people kept coming to see Dr. King. Streams of old men and women were arriving on foot from great distances, at once tired and tireless, but with a faith as old as the earth itself. There was no question in thier mind, Martin and Jesus were their saviors. And the living black whom all the world knew and sought, had found the time to visit their forgotten part of the world.

He looked very weary, but his eyes shone and his voice was strong and full of confidence. Andy was watching over him in a manner of one who is not watching anything at all. They had the signs and signals of those who know each other well and love each other much. I liked them immediately.

Darling, of course, stop reading any time you feel like it. But because your paper is due imminently, and my whole day is free, I'm going to write a great deal more than I generally do, so with that hiatus and warning, on we go.

A young man called me aside. He had been one of those turned away from the integrated school. But no one was turned away, I learned, if one or both of the parents accompanied the students to school. His parents, however, were afraid to go with him. I asked him what he would like me to do about it.

"Go and talk to my father. You're white and educated, so he'll listen to you." (Two of my worst qualifications, I thought).

I said: "When would you like me to go?"

"Now," he said.

His home, something more than a shack and less than a cabin, was a five minute walk from the church.

I was taken aback by the extraordinary austere beauty of the father, that beauty which only resignation and suffering can create and which one day, I hope, will no longer be seen in a human face.

I explained to him briefly about the school and his son's wishes. He nodded as I spoke. He understood. There was nothing, I was certain, that that man did not understand. He was Tolstoy's dream in American overalls: the peasant-aristocrat of the soil, the civilized man of inexpressible time-lessness.

"Nothing could happen to my position," he said, "because I have a federal job, but the white foreman would find out and make my life miserable. My wife's job doesn't matter to either of us. I'm sure she'll be willing to go."

"Good" I said, "Tell her we'll be meeting at the church at 8:30 in the morning."

"Thank you for caring about my son's education."

"Thank you for helping to educate me," I said, "That's not easy at my age."

"Why, you're still a young man."

I had forgotten—with my beard removed, I did look considerably younger, despite my Dachau pallor.

Back at the church we made plans for our nightly walk into town. It was to show that we were not afraid of the night, or of our white fellow citizens. I had not been in the church more than ten minutes when the young man whose father I had just spoken with, motioned to me. Anger made his lower lip tremble.

"My mother won't go to the school with me either."

"Why not?" I asked.

"As soon as you left the house, some one phoned and said that if either of them went with me, there would be a dead nigger in our house."

"My God!" I said, "they didn't waste much time. Who does the informing?"

"We don't know, but it happens all the time."

"We'll get you into the integrated school anyway," I said.

"I knew you would," he brightened. And curiously enough, we did. A most ambiguous favor.

That night, because of Dr. King's appearance there would be about four or five times the usual number of walkers. The sullen staff member, who detested Joan and me, did not like this either, but I had yet to discover what he did like save for the bourbon we drank together when the day's work was over.

Before the walk into town there was a mass rally at which almost all the SCLC staff spoke, with Dr. King last. Without exception, all the speakers sang as well as spoke. And what's more, they were good. A reporter from Newsweek magazine, sitting next to me, was as impressed as I.

"To be a high ranking civil rights worker," he said, "I guess you have to have an audition first."

When it was Dr. King's turn to speak everyone began stomping and clapping their hands.

"Tell us leader," many began to call out in unison. "Tell it, philosopher. Moses is here to deliver us from the house of bondage into the land of freedom."

Andy silenced the crowd by gently, unimposingly raising his hands. "Let us listen to what Dr. King has to tell us," he said.

"We will make a model city of Granada," Dr. King said. There were wild cheers.

"Yes, Granada will be a model city where little black children and little white children will go hand in hand. There'll be no poor man, black or white, who will be deprived of the fruits of his labor. In the heartland of Mississippi we will show the whole world that America is the land of the free and the home of the brave. Right here in Granada we will do this."

Ringing cheers reverberated on ringing cheers.

"Tell us, philosopher!"

"We shall overcome. And only by love and nonviolence shall we overcome. And if I'm the last black man in America, the last man in the world to think this, I shall never swerve from the straight and narrow path of truth and nonviolence.

"A friend is with us tonight who has often come to us in our need. I will ask Joan Baez, who has the voice of an angel, to sing for us."

Joan sang "Pilgrim of Sorrow." It was exquisite. The Newsweek reporter said to me: "If words, aspirations, and commitment could create a nonviolent world, we'd have it to-

136

night."

"We'll have it," I said, carried away from my usual skepticism, "It's the world's only chance of survival."

"I'd like to believe it," he said.

"Your children will see it."

"Sandperl, do you really believe that?"

"Tonight I do."

We were a great procession that evening when we walked into town. For a while I walked with the Newsweek man, for a while with Robert, the young field worker. He said: "Model city or no model city, I would just like to keep walking until we walk right out of this goddamn state."

"All right, I'm with you," I said, "but where will we go?"

"To Alabama," he said, and we both laughed.

I noticed a young girl walking alone, so I joined her.

"There are some very respectable folk out tonight," she said, good-humouredly. "I bet it's the first time they've ever walked anywhere."

"Lots of people walk for the first time when they are walking for their freedom," I said.

"Like Moses and the children of Israel?"

"Yes, and like you and me."

"But it ain't the first time we walked."

"No. And it won't be the last either." In my mind's eye I saw Gandhi, staff in hand, walking to the sea. Picking up a grain of salt with a beautiful movement of his arm and hand, he was nonviolently breaking the British monopoly of salt, its tax, its empire. His act, neither that of a politician, nor of a saint, was that of the most consummate artist. And with this signal, and by similar means, thousands upon thousands began transforming the prisons of India into the temples of India's freedom.

"Do you know about Mahatma Gandhi?" I asked my young walking companion.

"Yes," she assured me, she did: "He is a colored man, an Indian. He doesn't eat much. He prays a lot, uses a spinning wheel, and believes in nonviolence just like Dr. King, and he freed his people. Does he wear feathers?"

"No," I said, "just a pair of short pants that look like diapers, and a shawl over his shoulder if he ever got cold."

"What a funny Indian," the child said.

I agreed. "And like Dr. King, the whole world knew about him and loved him."

"Isn't he still living?"

"No, another Indian who, unlike Mr. Gandhi, thought that India should be a place where only one kind of Indian should rule over all other Indians killed him. The man who killed him wanted to go to war with another Indian country. He thought if Gandhi, who wanted all men to act like equals—like brothers—were dead, war would follow."

"Are you sure the man who killed Gandhi was really an Indian?"

"Yes, I'm sure."

"Well, he sure sounds like a white man."

We were approaching one of the two dangerous places on the walk. It was a small but thickly wooded area. Men could conceal themselves there, throw rocks and bottles at the walkers or shoot at them. I walked around my small partner in order to shield her in case any of these things happened. I thought I had done it easily, unobtrusively. But she immediately skipped around me to be on that side herself.

"Don't do that to an old man," I said lightly and again changed sides with her.

"But you're white," she said with great seriousness, "and they'll think you're a traitor."

"And you're black," I said with a smile, "and they'll think you're a nigger. There's not much difference, don't you agree?"

She laughed. Then very solemnly added: "You don't know these white Southern folks. In their eyes you're an outsider, a Northerner, a communist agitator, and I think to them that's even worse than being one of their own poor little niggers who don't know any better."

By this time we had passed the thicket of dark woods. We had almost the same conversation and the same maneuvering for position when we passed a section of low abandoned buildings, which was the other possible dangerous place. As she had done before, my little companion nimbly and embarrassingly outflanked me.

We reached the square which by then appeared like an armed encampment. To prepare for America's greatest apostle of nonviolence, the law and order advocates and their

138

minions exhibited a mammoth tableau of weaponry, fear and ignorance. It did not for a moment dampen the spirit of the multitude of walkers, for everyone, as soon as Joan began to sing, joined and filled the night with the exultation of freedom songs. Only the white men and their guns were silent.

I'm going to send you this, as promised, by Western Union. When my phone bill comes, I'll ask Joan to give me a benefit concert.

It was a great happiness talking to you on the telephone yesterday evening and hearing you tell me how much you liked the material on Martin Luther King. I'll confess to feeling briefly like some superannuated veteran telling of events he had taken part in a hundred years ago, whereas in fact, it was not all that long ago.

I am glad that what I have written will be of some use for your sociology paper. You said that your professor is flexible and unorthodox. That doesn't give me a clear picture of him, though I am certain that your paper will be more than acceptable. You have always been good at that sort of thing.

I'm really sorry that your *menage a trois* is suddenly going to pieces. If Thomas keeps "shooting up" with heroin and refuses to seek help, it is an impossible situation to deal with, especially if he is depressed most of the time and seldom even talks with you and Francis. It's peculiar, when I talked with him on the telephone, he was cheerful and optimistic about his drug and draft difficulties. Maybe he is "high" when he calls me, or feigns a special tone for our conversations.

Nevertheless, when you told me last night that he hasn't done anything about either predicament, I was not surprised. He must have consistently lied to me about both things, which is characteristic, in my experience, small though it is, with drug addicts. God, it's sad. And Thomas Warner is far from being stupid. I was a little wary because he kept saying precisely the things that pleased me the most on both subjects.

On the draft, without any conscious intimation from me, he told me he had decided that the only "meaningful" (his exact word) position was that of a total draft resister.

Concerning his heroin addiction he said he had found an excellent drug clinic at the Harvard Medical Center and had already made arrangements to be given treatments. He said he was enormously grateful to you, Francis and me, and, having made these decisions, he was happier than he'd ever been.

All lies, and all skillfully presented. Without having to

meet me, the boy intuited the perfect answers for me, all too perfect, as I have said.

And of course, I've grown generally fond of Thomas and would still be partially believing his stories had it not been for our telephone conversation last night. Perhaps when he was telling me these things he believed them himself. The charming person is at great disadvantage. He can generally accomplish what he sets out to do, and what he sets out to do, is usually, because of his charm, a psychological disaster, which he invariably discovers too late.

"Better never than late." That is G. B. Shaw, and I think it eminently clever, but not always true.

Cleverness, like charm, goes far, but in the wrong direction. In fact, it takes you swiftly backward like reels of film sped up and shown in reverse. It is great fun for a while, but only on a motion picture screen.

Three things I would wholeheartedly recommend not being, and I will list them in the order of their potential self-destructiveness: being a celebrity, being charming and being clever.

It would seem that one should be particularly watchful of words beginning with c's: catastrophe, calamity, cancer; but it is best not to add another superstition to this most superstitious age since early medieval times. And here I'm not in the least jesting.

SCIENCE, capitalizing each letter, is the enveloping superstition of our era, so it is humourously apt that your generation has flung astrology, tarot cards and the I Ching at the disapproving, science-soaked heads of your parents.

To each his own superstition. I wonder what your children will fling at you.

To return to Thomas, I don't know what to advise you. He tells me he is going to the Harvard Medical Center, and you—that he's off to Spain to escape the draft and have still easier access to heroin. Yet whatever his fantasies, his real circumstances will be changed by your and Francis' decision to separate. To put an end to what you now say should have never begun.

What you tell me sounds sad, right and considerate, as that kind of thing can be. Both of you will often be lonely as most people are, with or without companions. And both of you will doubtless regret many things, even though you know it's a damnable waste of energy; but you must remember that very few things are irreversible, and I like your idea of studying all about Tanzania and then going there to see what Nyerere is doing. I think Tanzania may well be one of the few original social experiments in existence. It is fascinating that your research on Dr. King should have led you in that direction.

Damn, it may be a ghastly world, but dull it is not. And of course, I'm glad I will be seeing you before you get immersed in your East African studies, and that will be soon.

Yesterday's letter was to be the last, in as much as I am going to see you in a few days.

But when I got your wire telling of Thomas' death by an overdose of heroin and/or suicide, I had to write, having been unable to reach you by telephone all morning. I shall keep telephoning you, but I will also send this letter by special delivery airmail. I choose not to wire this one.

God, how horrible to turn on the light in the bathroom and suddenly see Thomas' body there, prematurely old, wasted, dead.

Darling, there is nothing more to say to that particular sad young man. But there is much we can say and do for all the potential Thomas Warners of the world. For his was not an isolated problem, but a widespread social one, whether it was death by suicide or an accidental overdose. It is happening all the time, almost everywhere. And, I inferred from your wire that you were in some way blaming yourself, the decision you and Francis made to separate, and your not paying enough attention, perhaps, to Thomas.

At the risk of sounding self-righteous (but I can assure you that at this moment I don't feel a drop of self-righteousness), I do not think anyone could have prevented that boy from doing what he did. And if anyone could have, you would have been the one.

Only more experience and knowledge have yet to enter your incredible combination of intelligence and compassion. No mea culpa. Long ago, the Buddha pointed out that self blame is the most subtle form of egotism.

The heart has its reasons, and so does life, and they are, for the most part, a glory. There are, alas, a few things we all have to change: ourselves and our institutions, and each is as important as the other.

Your generation is on the move and there are many old folks striding alongside of you. We are going to make it.

I love you.

P.S. One astonishing 97-year-old man, who died only recently, and whose agelessness closed every generation gap said: "Kindliness and tolerance are worth all the creeds in the world." It was Bertrand Russell, and he was right.

The Last of
The Series

One of those extraordinary confirmations of faith (one is almost tempted to say miracles) occurred the other day when I opened the New York Times (the Talmud of the secular). It is the kind of confirmation which no one dares to seek, for in the very seeking it not only trivializes faith, but actually precludes it by making of it a vulgar act of calculated opportunism. Faith, on the other hand, is love's insight unbound by the fear of consequences.

In our attempts, personal and social, to diminish suffering, enhance life and let joy be the rainbow light in the tears of our eyes, we must know, as Gandhi always did, that it is what we think, feel, do and are which are the tools that make or mar our work. But all too often, understandably enough, we desire f fixed end product rather than the careful process of construction.

Yet our vision of a happier and more harmonious world lies solely in the quality of our ever-more refined actions, and those actions must never, in self-righteous impatience, be permitted to cloud our vision. Creating such a life seems laborious only in the insane context of our lightning capacity for destruction, which is in itself the very essence of well meaning but tragic impatience. Moreover, such a life is not a thing of burdensome duty, but one of high hopeful spirits. But let me not mislead you; it can also be one of frustration, sorrow, and dejection, not knowing whether you are being strong-minded or stubborn. And, there are times when you would like to run away, hide and never emerge from your room again. Even Christ in the garden of Gethesemane asked, "Let the cup pass from me," perhaps the most moving, the most human part of the new Testament. So there are times of floundering dejection when you behold yourself simultaneously longing for a new civilization while partially trapped in the old.

So in our frailty and temporary wavering, we are grateful for small and not so small victories whenever they arise. The example I'm about to relate fits perfectly into Gandhi's maxim, saying, "Full effort is full victory."

The young American men, calling themselves Resisters

who refused to cooperate in any way with military draft or to take part in the Vietnam war, and have gone to prison as a consequence, have done more than any group in this country to reverse the feelings and policies concerning this war. And they took this stand, not because they saw themselves as world transformers, but because they wanted to be responsible, moral and political human beings.

I now have a personal story to tell you of one resister who may have been responsible for literally changing the course of recent American history.

I was speaking on (against) the Vietnam War in Cambridge, Mass., to an audience which was comprised by and large of Harvard undergraduates. In the question period after my speech, a man, a good deal older than the rest, asked me a series of original, related questions concerning war, peace and power politics. His questions, in fact, were so unplatitiudinously stated, I facetiously asked, "Your questions are so thoughtful I'm going to have to think freshly about the answers for the first time in years. Who the hell are you?"

Very seriously, he said, "I am a disciple of a disciple of yours."

"I have no disciples," I said.

"Well, there is a young man in a federal prison in Texas," he went on to say, "who is there because he refused unconditionally to go into the United States Army. He told the presiding judge of his case that he would not allow himself to be involved in any organization that has anything to do with the deliberate taking of a single human life, and that includes being a killer without a gun, such as a typist, or file clerk, or medic. And because of his remarkably political and humane stand, I am strongly influenced to take a similar action. And this young man says he wouldn't be in his present situation if it hand't been for knowing you."

I was going to answer the man's questions and talk a little of my gentle, intelligent and humorous friend, Randy Kehler, who is serving three years in the Texas prison. But the students hurriedly began asking me many questions about the draft, so I was diverted from my original questioner.

However, when the meeting was over the same man and his wife approached me and asked if I could have dinner with them. I told them I was sorry (they seemed appealingly serious, quiet and modest) but I had to get to the airport to fly to my next speaking engagement. They asked if they could drive me to the airport and I happily accepted. All the way there, until I boarded the jet, the man kept asking me what it was like for middle class men such as ourselves to spend time in jail. I answered him as best I could (explaining that I had been in jail a number of times for nonviolent civil disobedience, but never for more than forty-five days). Yet I could not help wondering what was worrying this smartly dressed professor. We had exchanged names very rapidly, but I had already forgotten his when I was on the plane with my Bloody Mary and the notes for my next speech.

Well, a few days ago I saw the man's photograph in the New York Times under a lead article entitled, "The Pentagon Papers." It was obvious that the man I had met was Daniel Ellsberg.

Randy Kehler's truth was stronger than all the resources of the most powerful government on earth.

D
ear M? Dearest M? Darling?

Damn! After two years of the barest contact and the most frugal correspondence, I do not know how to begin a letter to you that does not sound too formal, too self-conscious, or too familiar. To avoid my discomfort, at least momentarily, I will first comment on your three cheers for the ending of the war in Indo-China.

Alas, we cannot give those three cheers, for the simple, unspeakable fact that the war in Indo-China is not over. With or without the so-called truce, with or without American troops, the fighting goes on: death by bullet, grenade, mortar, disease and starvation continues. Refugee camps swell and large areas of a once beautiful countryside are pitted with sterile bomb craters.

Nixon's Peace with Honor coupled with the largest military budget in the history of the world turns out to be more ferociously cynical than Chamberlain's Peace in Our Time.

Nor can we cheer that the criminal barbarism of American bombing in Cambodia stopped on August 15. For not even from a military point of view was there even any justification for it. Nevertheless, ashamed, disgusted, disgraced and contrite we of course welcomed its cessation.

But other countries are also at war within as well as without: the Middle East, Ghana, Ethiopia, Mozambique, the Sudan, Ireland, Greece, Uruguay, Brazil, Chile and on and on and on. The number is distressingly legion. And everywhere more military dictatorships are coming into existence (a surety for future wars) in an attempt to cope with the exhorbitant costs of living, poverty, national pride and overpopulation. At the same time they are continually maneuvering to build a collective bloc in a frantic drive to keep divided the unholy trinity of the U.S.A., the U.S.S.R. and China.

Peace has become the marching banner to distract civilians and to mobilize armies.

Does this bleak picture mean that we who are committed to the social organization of nonviolence have no place? On the contrary, we have much work and much hope.

The Pentagon Papers, themselves a result of the anti-Vietnam war movement, particularly the nonviolent wing (see the press statements of Daniel Ellsberg) have begun to lay bare the dark citadel of America's authorized violence and calculated treachery. Following this, the Watergate affair, if pursued vigorously, scrupulously and to its roots, could mean the reversal of the entire totalitarian process which has been gathering sinister momentum since the First World War. But the Watergate investigation must stop talking of the abuses of power of the Army, the C.I.A., the F.B.I. and the presidency and understand that such organizations are, by their very nature, an abuse of power.

Furthermore, we must, on pain of universal death, translate Gandhi's adherence to truth, love, and nonviolence (Satyagraha) into specific local and world-wide political, economic, social and spiritual programs.

Hannah Arendt in her admirable and important book, the *Orgins of Totalitarianism,* states that we must devise a political principle that will this time cover every man, woman and child on earth. The principle is Satyagraha. We have to study it seriously, develop it imaginatively and practice it conscientiously. And we can do it, provided, of course, that we want to do it.

Then we will be able to give three of the loveliest and most resounding cheers.

To return to my personal malaise as I once again find myself writing to you at length and let me admit that I am a trifle chagrined and somewhat saddened that I should feel any such disquiet in my relationship to you.

Time, distance, silence and separation are not the facile scapegoats we would like to make them. No, my love of blessed and ghostly memory, it is ourselves. And it is not consciences that make cowards of us all, but our pathetic need of a touching, breathing, living presence, the tangible that we can behold and hold.

Surely you live on in some remote, quiet, faithfully tended chamber of my mind, elegant and unflawed, brushing your glorious hair, with fresh roses on the table and geraniums in the window box; but in truth the setting is too much like one of those rooms in a museum roped off by heavy velvet cords which people glance at but seldom enter.

Yet I am confident were we to meet in your Tanzanian village or on the streets of San Francisco, our hands would once more discover that separation is but one of the cruelest and most tormenting illusions.

In closing, I want to thank you for returning the letters I wrote to you and for giving your enthusiastic consent to having them published.

I was amused by your remark that you thought every young woman should have a Sandperl education, but that you had had yours.

Did you have to be so emphatic in your use of the pluperfect tense?

Ciao and love,

Ira's Annotated Book List

PART I

These are a handful of the master magicians who turned words into reality instead of, like most of us, turning reality into words. I have lited, in most cases, one or more of their works, though I would suggest reading them all.

Aristophanes, **Frogs**—(B. B. Rogers' translation.) All of his great comedies, with humor which has not been dimmed by time, throw more light on the ancient Greeks than the would-be weightier Tragedians.

Aeschylus, **Persians**—(The Lattimore translation.) Neither the Persians nor the Greeks nor the rest of the world have taken seriously that which Aeschylus makes abundantly clear; i.e., that Hubris (overweening pride) always and everywhere results in nemesis (retribution, vengeance).

Sophocles, **Antigone**—(The Lattimore Translation.) This develops the lonely, moral grandeur of a single woman defying the might of an empire and the superstitions of a culture.

Euripides, **Trojan Women**—(Edith Hamilton translation.) If art could have put an end to war this play would have done it. Only Goya's *"Disasters of War"* may be more powerful.

*William Shakespeare-*It's arrogant to attempt to list only two of his works; however, with this said, my suggestions are **Measure for Measure** and **King Lear.**

*William Blake-*Blake's vision, at once red hot and ice cold, never faltered. His poetry, unlike that of any others', is the language of life and death for, as it has been said, he dared "The Marriage of Heaven and Hell."

Dante Alighieri, **The Divine Comedy**—If Shakespeare is the supreme fox of literature (surveying everything), Dante is the supreme hedgehog (Dante's single vision not only permeated but transcended all of the later Middle Ages in an Italian that was close enough to Latin so it could be read beyond his native borders). "The fox knows many things, but the hedgehog knows one big thing."—*Archilochus,* Greek poet of the 7th century, B.C.

*Johann Wolfgang Von Goethe-***Faust** Parts I and II. (George Madison Priest translation.) Goethe delineates in searing language the aspirations, the exhaltations, the prejudices and the baseness of Western culture.

Cervantes, **Don Quixote—**(The Putnam translation) Dostoevsky called it the Bible of the world. It's funnier, sadder, saner and more humane than the Bible with which most of us are allegedly familiar.

Leo Tolstoy, **Anna Karenina—**(Louise and Aylmer Maude translation.) Tolstoy saw these translations and approved.) Although *Anna Karenina* is concerned with a woman in the Russian Society of the 19th century, the book contains, with incredible intensity, all the things with which men, women and children have always been concerned. In some ways his more famous novel, **War and Peace**, has much the same attributes, but what he loses in intensity here, he makes up for in the vast panorama he puts forth. Moreover, miraculously enough, no character is duplicated in either book.

Fyodor Dostoevsky, **The Brothers Karamazov** (Constance Garnett translation.) At first reading the book appears so wild and deranged that it seems out of our ordinary experience. On second reading, it seems closer to life than anything we are ever likely to read. **Memoirs from the House of Dead—**(David Magarahack translation.) This is an account of Dostoevsky's year in Siberia. It will be timely and poignant so long as men are imprisoned anywhere.

*Michel De Montaigne-*The French have a happy way of making their classics not only first rate but delightfully readable. Unpretentious and casual, Montaigne lets us know in the simplest language what it is to be civilized. His third book of essays is the best. Yet my experience is that once this is read, one will eagerly seek to read his entire works.

*Marcel Proust-*His major work **Remembrance of Things Past** might easily be compared to the best of the Russian

154

novels. He saw everything, felt everything, and understood everything, and was able to convey it to those of us measurelessly less endowed. I would add to this incredible work a book entitled **Marcel Proust—Chosen and Translated by Gerald Hopkins.** This and Proust's earliest publication, **Pleasures and Days,** comprise most of the author's shorter pieces. They show him warming up for his **Magnum Opus** and a very impressive warm-up it is. To savor further this remarkable man and his times, I would suggest reading George D. Painter's two-volume biography **Proust, The Early Years** and **Proust, The Later Years.** Proust's countryman and fellow writer of belles lettres, Andre Maurois, has written a good, one-volume biography.

Francois Rabelais, **Gargantua and Pantagruel**—This 16th century French physician, humanist and satirist produced the most extraordinary, vivacious and rollicking picture (one would like to use the adjective Rabelaisian) of French society in all its tumbling variety. It's as serious, and possibly even funnier, than **Don Quixote.**

Franz Kafka, **The Trial.** In this book, alarmingly, everyone recognizes his or her own trial. **The Complete Short Stories** (published by Shocken). Here we find a world of fantasy that our century has turned into one aspect of grim reality. **Conversations With Kafka.** The conversations he has with the nineteen-year-old poet Janorich bring forth a gentle, infinitely considerate Kafka, an admixture of extraordinary strength and self-effacement.

Lao Tzu, **The Way of Life According to Lao Tzu** (The Witter Bynner translation.) **The Way and Its Power** (The Arthur Waley translation.) Both these books are translations of the Chinese **Tao Tê Ching,** and together they comprise that one perfect volume for the desert island or the subway. In these uncertain days, it would be wise to have at least one of these volumes with you at all times. Shelley had in his pocket a copy of Sophocles when he drowned.

Bhagavad Gita—This is a long sanskirt poem incorporated into the longer work of the Mahabharata. The *Gita* is the most popular devotional book of the Hindus, of both the simple and the sophisticated. There are many translations, but the most readable for us is the one done by Christopher Isherwood and Swami Prabhavananda.

In Gandhi's library, this book held a pride of place inasmuch as its central teaching is his; that our concern should always be primarily with our labor, never with the fruits of our labor. In short, the means are absolutely everything and the ends are dependent, if not wholly identical with, the means we use.

Attributed to Buddha-**The Dhammapada** (translation by Irving Babbitt.) Of all the beautiful, simple and complex volumes on Buddhism, this one has the advantage of being lucid and straightforward. It not only tells us of the necessity of wise social ethics, but also of the grounding that can make those ethics a reality.

Jalal al-Din Rumi-**The Masnavi** (The Arberry translation.) The original in Persian and the translation by A. J. Arberry rank, by common consent, among the world's greatest masterpieces of religious literature. Anecdotes, parables and poetry; sublime.

Thomas à Kempis, **The Imitation of Christ**—14th century Christianity was a remarkably productive time and this little book is one of its finest offerings, "All men desire peace," Thomas à Kempis tells us, "but few men desire these things which make for peace."

The Apocrypha—The contents of this volume were excluded from the Bible, perhaps God only knows why. They are all of great interest, particularly the Wisdom of Solomon.

Karl Marx and Fredrick Engels, **The Communist Manifesto**—This is in the great tradition of the Hebrew prophets. The vision, the drama and the self-righteousness stream forth as a not minor addition of the Old Testament.

PART II

The following is but an infinitesmal sampling of the apprentice magicians. And like many apprentices, a stroke of theirs here and there is more brilliant than the masters.

Jonathan Swift, **Gulliver's Travels** and **The Tale of a Tub—**If you read these and thought they were children's stories, read them again.

Samuel Butler, **Erewhon** and **Erewhon Revisited.** Despite the title, Erewhon is not a mythical place. It is England in the 19th century and although England and we have changed, it's only to have partially caught up with Butler's meditations which, incidentally, are some of the funniest in the English language. **The Way of All Flesh—**Here, once and for all, we see family life as we all tremblingly know it. It makes Albee's "Who's Afraid of Virginia Woolf?" seem like a comedy of domestic good manners.

Italo Suevo, **A Man Grows Older, A Life, The Confessions of Zeno,** and **Further Confessions of Zeno** are novels of heartbreaking beauty.

Cesare Pavese, **The House on the Hill** and **Among Women Only** are two of this flinty man's finest books. **The Burning Brand** is the title of the remarkable diaries he kept from 1935 to 1950. In 1950 Pavese received Italy's major literary prize, Premio Strega, after which he took his life.

*Alexander Sergeevich Pushkin-*The father, if not the grandfather, of all great Russian literature. Nortan Press publishes his complete stories and prose. There are many editions of his long, moving poem, **"Eugene Onegin."**

*Anton Chekhov-*His plays **"The Seagull," "Uncle Vanya," "The Three Sisters"** and **"The Cherry Orchard"** are 19th century Russian-set pieces which have, curiously enough, touched the hearts and minds of subsequent generations throughout the world. His short stories are perhaps even better; more authentic than those of that superb artist de Maupassant.

*Thomas Mann-*Read all of his fiction, from **Buddenbrooks** to **Confessions of Felix Krull, Dr. Faustus** and **The Magic**

Mountain. In varying colors, he depicts our time's superficial delusions and tragic defeats.

Bertolt Brecht–His **Mother Courage, St. Joan of the Stockyard, The Caucasian Chalk Circle, The Good Woman of Setzuan,** and **Galileo** are all dramatically concerned with means and ends, circumstances and responsibility. Also his book of poetry, **Manual of Piety,** should be read.

Ralph W. Emerson–He is often talked about and more often ridiculed and consistently less read than many of his lesser compatriots. Yet Emerson, Melville, and Whitman still have much to say to our world. Only Emerson's most common essays (not that they aren't good) are available, even in most libraries. Perhaps there will be a revival of his work as there has been periodically of that of Henry James. Any of the writings of the above-mentioned authors will not be a waste of anyone's time.

George Santayana–**The Last Puritan.** This elegant Spanish and American philosopher wrote only this one work of fiction. It may be his best work, as well as the most accurate reading of the American soul.

Goustave Flaubert– His most widely read and one time notorious book is **Madame Bovary.** It's a moving work of ambitious, provincial France, though he went on to do different and better things in **Sentimental Education, Three Tales** and **Bouvard and Pecuchet.** His earliest novel, **November,** makes interesting reading, as does his **Intimate Notebook 1840-1841.** Recently published is **Flaubert in Egypt,** which is a translation of letters and journals which are both observant and amusing. Enid Starkie's two-volume biography of Flauert is vintage Stariie: **I The Marking of the Master, II Flaubert the Master.**

Andre Malraux– **The Voices of Silence.** With unwonted timidity, Edmund Wilson thought this probably was one of the greatest books of the 20th century. There was absolutely no cause for Mr. Wilson's timidity, except that he did not write it himself. The translation is by Stuart Gilbert. Also his **Man's Fate** may be not only the best political novel of our time, but also may surpass in intelligence all the recent plethord of books that have been written on China. His penultimate book **Anti-Memoir** gives an astute look at the political forces crowding in on us today, as well as some of thier antecedents.

Karl Kraus-To date there is nothing translated of this man's fantastically original satirical work. I cannot believe, difficult as such a translation would be, that this will not be done soon. Kraus, as an iconoclast and a polemicist has few, if any equals. He influenced people from Schoenberg to Wittenstein. As an example of his style, he wrote that "Vienna was a proving ground for world destruction." Another example is "Psychoanalysis is that spiritual disease of thich it considers itself to be the cure."

Robert Musil-**The Man Without Qualities.** In this book perhaps more than any other novel set in pre-World War I Vienna, we are able to see the conflicting seeds, good and bad, that have flowered in our century.

Chuang Tzu-**Chuang Tzu** is both the name of a Taoist philosopher and Chinese mystic as well as the title of his work. This man of the 3rd and 4th centuries before Christ was either the wisest humorist who ever lived or the most humorist wise man. Herbert A. Giles gives, to date, the best translation of the writings of this wholly delightful man.

Wu Ch'eng-en-**Monkey.** This is an extraordinary 16th century Chinese masterpiece. **Monkey** represents human cleverness without the realization of the Buddha nature. His adventures are comic, michievous, ingenious, and ultimately self-destructive. Its lightness of tone makes its timeless impact all the more inescapable.

Kadhakrishnan and Thoore-**A Source Book in Indian Philosophy.** I'm usually wary of general survey books of this sort, but his is a superb and full picture of Indian thought with specific sources given and admirably translated and historically documented.

Sri Aurobindo-**The Life Divine.** The admirers of de Chardin will find Aurobindo has developed a synthesis that makes **The Phenomenon of Man** seem like a kiddy's primer of the spiritual life.

Lady Murasaki **The Tale of the Genji.** This is a novel in six parts written in Japan's 10th century. It is as sophisticated as any of the great European 18th century works. It has often been compared in minutiae, subtly and in depth to Marcel Proust's **Remembrance of Things Past.** The only adverse criticism I've heard of it is that Japanese scholars have remarked that Arthur Waley's excellent English translation is a little better than the original.

D. T. Suzuki-**Zen and Japanese Culture.** The writing and the illustrations of this book make the Western view of Japan one long inconsequential platitude.

Julio Cortazar-**Cronopios and Famas.** Cortazar's work has the fantasy of reality and the waking quality of dreams.

Jorge Luis Borges-**Labyrinths.** This book consists of a selection of stories and essays that have appeared in the last forty years. He has the poet's genius in making manifest the simple and the obvious which most of us never see, and that genius includes the strictest economy of expression.

Garcia Marquez-**One Hundred Years of Solitude.** To those of us who are not familiar with the South American landscape, much unusual beauty will be revealed; however, the passions and aspirations in this novel, although vigorous and unsentimental, will in no way seem strange.

Camara Laye-**The African Child.** This autobiography resounds throughout the whole world of the dispossessed.

Frantz Fanon-**Black Skin, White Mask.** Fanon deals specifically with the blacks as a psychological and historical prey of the white world, and at the same time he offers a way out of this mutually destructive relationship. In my opinion, the importance of the book lies in the fact that he makes clear the urgency, perhaps on the pain of universal death, of the removal of all idealogical and national masks. The writing is bitingly beautiful.

Plato-**Collected Dialogues.** Edited by Edith Hamilton and Huntington Cairns. These are the most important Platonic dialogues in their best English translations.

F. M. Cornford-**Before and After Socrates.** A tiny, exquisite volume that tells more of Greek thought than all the ponderous tomes on the subject.

Werner Jaeger-**Paideia: The Ideals of Greek Culture.** A three-volume work which gives you the clearest sense of what the ancient Greeks were all about.

E. R. Dodds-**The Greeks and the Irrational.**Professor Dodds shows the primitive and irrational forces which operate and give shape to this highly sophisticated society.

Seneca-**The Stoic Philosophy.** In these essays and letters we discover the origins of the life and thought patterns that have become a part of every culture.

Epicurus, Epictetus, Lucretius, and Marcus Aurelius. **The Stoic and Epicurean Philosophers.** (The original sources) is assembled in one volume by W. J. Oakes. As usual, it is between the lines that we perceive slave and citizen trying to create some order out of the growing chaos of the later Roman times.

Spinoza-**Ethics.** Although much of his formulation would ill fit our times, the powerful affirmative spirit animating this great work is one of the things for which we have a pressing need.

Arthur Schopenhauer-**Essays and Aphorisms.** (Penguin Publication.) Too long has our century simply dismissed Shcopenhauer as a pessimist. His insight into creative resignation and the awareness of one's limitations, have and will always have a compelling relevance to man. He's also a writer of the first rank.

Ludwig Wittgenstein-**Tractatus Logico Philosophicus.** To date there is no adequate English translation of this work which, in my amateur estimation, has close affinity with Lao Tzu's **Toa Teh Ching.** The silences that ring through the Chinese sage's small volume ring also through the last part of the **Tractatus.** Wittgenstein, like Loa Tzu, knew that the unsayable could only be suggested and hinted at.

Sigmund Freud-**Civilization and Its Discontents.** We may often disagree with the observations in this book, but it would be hard to deny that it has had and has a widespread impact, consciously or unconsciously, on our world.

F. W. Myers-**Human Personality and Its Survival of Bodily**

Death. If Freud has exhumed the dark and sordid chambers of our mind, Myers explores perhaps the even deeper passage-ways of light and freshness.

Chinese Poems. Translation by Arthur Waley. In this volume Waley has included almost all of his translations of the great Chinese poems. I know of nothing in any language simpler, more striking and beautiful.

*C. P. Cavafy-***The Complete Poems of C. P. Cavafy.** Not knowing a word of modern Greek, it is not only difficult, but also presumptious to comment on this work. Cervantes once said that translations were like viewing tapestries from the hidden side. In short, the colors, the nuances, and the delicacy, all are missing. Nevertheless, I would maintain there is yet not a work that, as the Quakers say, "speaks to our condition" as marvelously as those that Carvafy has wrought (even in translation).

From Copernicus to Einstein by *Hans Reichenbach,* **One, Two, Three . . . Infinity** by *George Gamow,* **The ABC of Relativity** by *Bertrand Russell,* and **Physics and Politics** by *Max Born.* All of these books give us in non-technical language the principles, and effects of the physical sciences.

*Loren Eiceley-***The Immense Journey.** This book puts nature and all of us in our place. And we discover that our place is multiple and as beautiful as it is bewildering.

*Harlow Shapely-***Of Stars and Men.** The galaxies are brought closer and we can see ourselves in perspective.

*H. G. Wells-***The Outline of History.** Though Mr. Well's book was written in 1920, his opening sentence still has real validity in spite of the nuclear revolution. He says it "is an attempt to tell truly and clearly, in one continuous narrative, the whole story of life and mankind so far as it's known today."

*Edward Gibbon-***Decline and Fall of the Roman Empire.** In spite of the all too facile analogies relating our idea to that of the Roman Empire, this magnificantly written three-volume history could aid us in coming to grips with the entire suicidal concept of empire and its consequences.

162

Aristotle-**The Politics.** Wherever one begins or ends in the strivings, ideals and chaos of the body politic, one must start and return to the tutor of Alexander the Great.

Hannah Arendt-**The Origins of Totalitarianism.** I wish this book were easier to read because it's a handbook we should carry with us always. It not only raises all the overwhelming questions of the day, but answers them with the lucidity and intelligence that we have unhappily ignored.

J. Krishnamurti-**Education and the Significance of Life.** Heartbreakingly, this is the way education could be, but so far as I know, has never been. The age-old task remains—by whom and how are the educators to be educated?

The Teacher and the Taught: Education in Theory and Practice from Plato to James B. Conant. Lively contrary disquisitions, at times abrasive, but gloriously lacking the stuffiness of a classroom.

The Life and Work of Sigmund Freud by *Ernest Jones,* **Karl Marx** by *Franz Mehring,* **Charles Darwin** by *Sir Gavin DeBeer.* Without knowing the life and thoughts of these three men, we will be further victimized by not knowing what formed and still forms, for good and for ill, our age. And for those of you who will live into the 21st century, you would do well to know of the lives and thoughts of Max Plank (the Quantam Theory), Albert Einstein (the general and special theories of relativeiy), and Mahatma Gandhi (the principle method of resisting oppression without spilling blood and the means to carry out radical social change without violence).

M. K. Gandhi-**My Experiments with Truth.** This autobiography is doubtless the most scrupulous that has ever been written. Unlike most works, particularly autobiographies, truth with a small t is the central nagging character.